Exploring
TEXTILE ARTS

The **ULTIMATE** guide to manipulating, coloring, and embellishing fabrics

Creative Publishing
international

Minneapolis, Minnesota

Exploring
TEXTILE ARTS

The **ULTIMATE** guide to manipulating,
coloring, and embellishing fabrics

Creative Publishing
international

President/CEO: Ken Fund
VP Sales & Marketing: Kevin Hamric

Created by: The Editors of Creative Publishing international, Inc.

Printed in China
10 9 8

Library of Congress Cataloging-in-Publication Data

Exploring textile arts : the ultimate guide to manipulating, coloring, and
embellishing fabrics.
    p. cm.
   Includes index.
   ISBN 1-58923-048-5 (soft cover)
   1. Textile crafts. 2. Textile design. 3. Textile painting. 4. Textile printing.
   5. Dyes and dying--Textile fabrics. I. Creative Publishing International.

TT699 .E94 2002
746--dc21   2002017369

Diane Bartels

CONTENTS

INTRODUCTION

Calling all fabric lovers! Prepare to embark on a new journey of artistic discovery in a world where you design fabrics to fit your imagination. In the realm of fabric artistry, fabric is selected for its merits as an open canvas, waiting for an inspired hand to alter its character and define its purpose. Surface texture, color, print design, and hand are traits that you, the artist, can change and develop in the creative process.

Breathe fresh energy into your sewing projects, whether they be quilts, home décor, garments, or gifts. Learn how to build depth and character with manipulation techniques, like felting, pleating, texturizing, quilting, trapunto, and devoré. Color your fabrics with fiber-reactive dyes and fabric paints, transforming your ideas into visually captivating cloth. With user-friendly methods like screen printing, stenciling, or stamping, develop interesting patterns that reflect your own personality. Use your new creations or found fabrics as backgrounds for expressive free-motion machine embroidery or fanciful appliqués. Stud the fabric surface with beadwork or add glimmering foil accents.

(continued)

INTRODUCTION (continued)

We invite you to admire and muse over the many splendid exhibits in the Artists' Galleries, each expressing unique personality and style. The fabrics, techniques, and embellishments used for each project are the personal choices made by each artist. Take inspiration from these artists, knowing that their creations are the results of their own journeys of artistic discovery.

During your exploration, use the instructions and photographs as a springboard to designing your own unique fabrics. Allow yourself the luxury of experimenting with a wide range of techniques, understanding that you may take an instant dislike to some and be immediately enthralled with others.

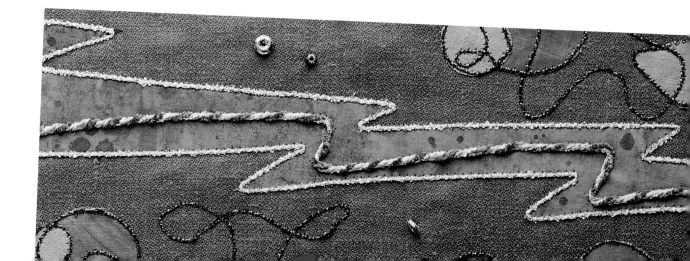

Turn undesirable results into positive experiences; consider mistakes to be valuable learning tools to help you make choices. But be warned; this creative play can lead to addiction. There are no limits to your enjoyment, and once your journey of fabric artistry explorations begins, you may find time for little else!

Acknowledgment

We wish to express our sincere gratitude to the fabric artists who so generously allowed us to photograph their creations. Thank you for sharing your ideas, your dreams, and your talents as inspiration for our readers.

Part 1:
TEXTURE & DEPTH

Artists'
GALLERY #1

■ ■

Look for inspiration in
unexpected places.
Train your eyes to see the
possibilities that
hide beneath realities.

C arol Sperling created this hand-felted vest and hat, using dyed fleece, bits of old wool sweaters, and blanket fabric. She has specialized in making hand-felted hats, booties, and mittens for over a decade. Interested in spinning, knitting, and weaving, Carol is fascinated by antique looms and has instituted a demonstration program near Chisholm, Minnesota, at Iron World, a museum that celebrates the ethnic settler groups of this logging and iron-ore mining area. Members of Carol's fiber-arts guild demonstrate rag rug and fabric weaving on Scandinavian-style looms each summer.

CAROL SPERLING

KATHERINE TILTON

K atherine Tilton is the designer of this felted wool coat. It features raw-edge appliqué and hand-painted binding. Katherine designs eclectic hand-painted clothing and objects, which have appeared in many exhibitions and collections. She has taught art and art-to-wear classes for children in public schools and through the St. Paul Museum of American Art. She has also created and taught art classes and workshops for adults, served as a consultant on several Singer® Sewing Reference Library® books, and worked with the COMPAS/Minnesota Coalition for Battered Women Open Book Project, where she developed the model for an art project and statewide exhibition for children in shelters.

LIN LACY

Lin Lacy, a fiber artist, "paints" in multimedia, creating wall hangings, art clothing and decorative objects. She has worked in interior design, created theater costumes, and restored museum tapestries. Lin is known for her use of recycled clothing, jewelry, and household items to create unique wearable art, adorned with appliqué, beading, and embroidery. This winter ensemble exhibits Lin's creative knack with felted wool, couched yarns, and beading.

Gini Corrick designed this silk blouse, which features texturized fabric with decorative stitching and beadwork. Gini describes herself as a "sewist," having had a love affair with fabric since childhood. In addition to participating in and twice serving as director of the Airstream International Rally Fashion Show, Gini has organized sewing seminars for that group and has conducted annual wearable art shows.

GINI CORRICK

JANE CONLON

■ ■ ■ ■ ■ ■ ■ ■ ■ ■ ■ ■ ■ ■ ■ ■ ■ ■

Jane Conlon sews, writes, and teaches in the Pacific Northwest. Enchanted with the practical and creative challenges that sewing provides, she consistently strives for artfulness that is apparent in the attention to detail and workmanship of the garment. Her techniques include fabric weaving, machine-stitched and hand-stitched embroidery, appliqués, and beadwork embellishments. This pin-woven vest is a prime example of her ability to work decorative details into the garment design. Some of Jane's work, including the Celtic appliqué and trapunto designs below, has appeared in *Threads* magazine.

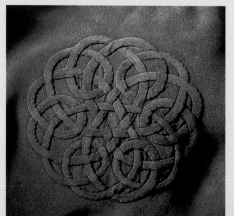

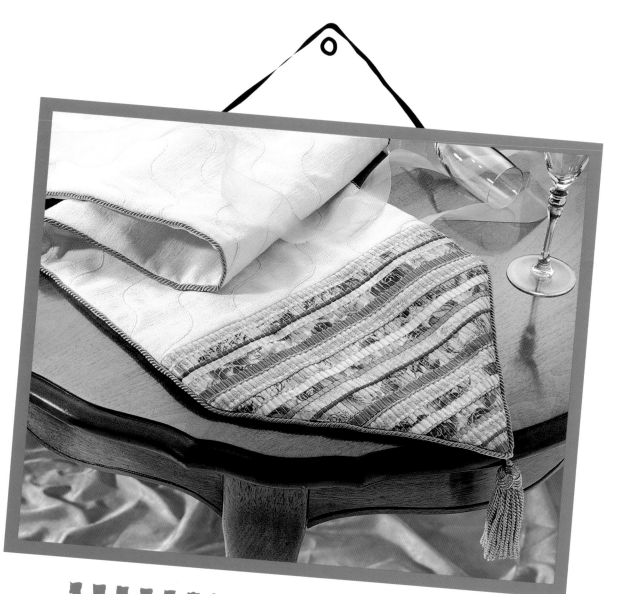

P in weaving and double-needle stitching are combined in this elegant table runner, designed and sewn by members of our staff. Fabric artistry techniques give home fashions designer appeal while giving your decorating scheme a personal touch.

Julann Windsperger, who has been sewing since before she started school, has combined a 25-year nursing career with a home-based business, Julann's Stitchery. Since 1990, she has been creating unique quilted and pieced garments, like the one at left. Julann works nights in a hospital transplant unit and days designing and stitching on her industrial quilting machine—as she says, "What excitement!" Julann's work is also featured on page 119.

JULANN WINDSPERGER

LINDA NELSON BRYAN

Linda Nelson Bryan is an award-winning textile artist with a Masters degree in Textile Design. Her works encompass an amalgam of varied surface design techniques and aesthetic approaches. In this dress, Linda has combined various dyeing techniques with a rhythmic flowing cascade of double-needle pintucks. Linda has exhibited internationally and has participated in a number of artist residencies, including several years with COMPAS and a summer spent at the Fiberarts Interchange at the Banff Centre for the Arts, Canada. For several years, she has taught college courses in Surface Design and Fiber Structure.

PENELOPE TRUDEAU

Penelope D. Trudeau took an early retirement, after a long career in hospital management and a degree in law, to devote her time to quilting. She creates wall quilts and garments in order to express herself through fiber and "bring art and beauty. . . peace and calm. . .into other people's lives." Her art, represented by the coat at left, combines original design, fabric painting and dyeing, and many needlework skills. She agrees with a friend, who said, "There is no finer place to show art than on your back!" Penelope's work is also featured on page 118.

Justine Limpus Parish has worked in the fashion industry as an illustrator, art director, designer, and educator. She created the Fashion Department at the Academy of Art College in San Francisco, lectures and teaches workshops on Innovative Design, and is the author of *Drawing the Fashion Body.* She currently produces a line of Shibori hand-pleated and color-accented garments, such as this coat and dress ensemble, featured in specialty stores nationwide.

JUSTINE LIMPUS PARISH

JOAN WIGGINTON

J oan Kees Wigginton, a
professional interior designer,
started sewing on her grandmother's
Singer® treadle machine,
beginning with doll's clothes
and later designing gowns for
friends' high school
dances. She has taught
adult education sewing-
construction classes
and continues to design
clothes and explore new
materials and design details. Her
jacket was inspired by her love of diving into
the undersea world and by the book, *Quilted Sea
Tapestries*, by Ginny Eckley.

24

MARIAN HEHRE

Marian Hehre began sewing at an early age, influenced by her grandmother. An avid quilter since 1982, Marian has gradually moved from traditional styles to wearable art, as demonstrated by her unique jackets, here and on page 2. She teaches a variety of classes to all ages and has won several awards for her designs. A common thread through all of Marian's activities is her ability to move herself and others beyond traditional boundaries, view mistakes as creative opportunities, and truly enjoy the creative process.

BARB PRIHODA

Barb Prihoda is fascinated by the unlimited possibilities of free-motion machine embroidery. When she is not up at the lake or spending time with her family, Barb enjoys experimenting with new techniques and developing her own designs. Her award-winning work has appeared in *The Creative Machine Newsletter, Sewing Update,* and Mary Mulari's book, *More Sweatshirts With Style*. She has been a featured guest on "Sewing With Nancy," in a three-part series entitled "Carefree Machine Embroidery." Barb enjoys sharing her ideas with other machine-embroiderers around the country.

CORALIE SATHRE

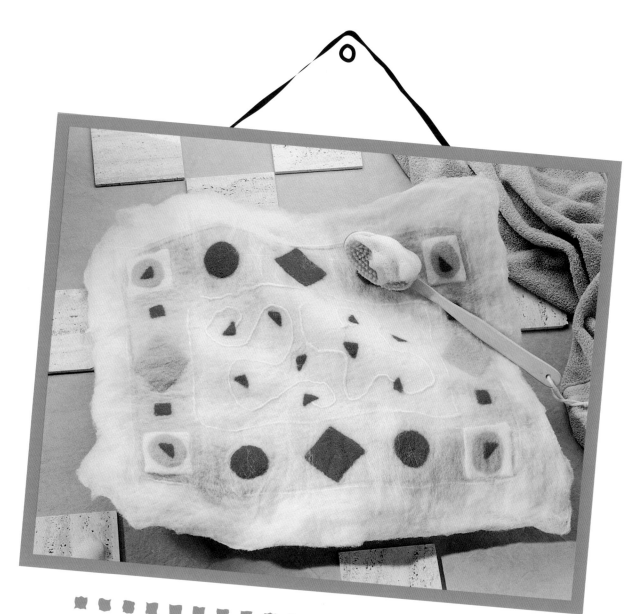

C oralie Sathre designed and felted this wool bath rug. Making felted wool is a new venture for her, one that seems to be a natural fit, considering her degree in Fine Arts and her love for the tactile and visual pleasures of fiber arts. Among her many interests, Coralie enjoys hand knitting and loom weaving.

E mbossed rayon velvet edged with opulent bullion fringe gives this window swag a look of total elegance. The swag was designed, embossed, and sewn by members of our sewing staff.

IRIS LEE

I ris Lee, who began sewing on a treadle machine, taught fine arts, crafts, and needlework for 20 years before realizing the "infinite possibilities" of the new computerized machines, new threads, and new techniques of machine embroidery; she envisions a creative linkup between the personal computer and the sewing machine. She has taught her cutwork and decorative techniques since 1990 and has described them in two books; *Threads* magazine; and a video, "Artwork & Needlelace."

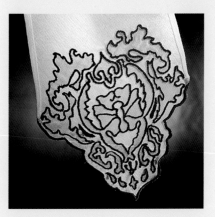

Random-cut fabric weaving and quilted effects were among the techniques used by members of our sewing and design staff to create this luxurious wool pillow. Their concerted efforts produced a celebration of textures, colors, and fabric artistry.

MARGARET ANDOLSHEK

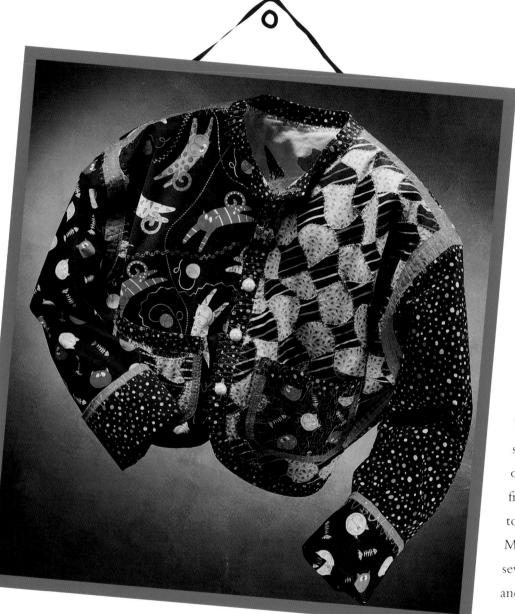

M argaret Andolshek began sewing when she was nine years old. After moving from the East Coast to the Midwest, Margaret joined several sewing clubs and began taking sewing and fabric-manipulation classes. She continually challenges herself to try new techniques and shares her knowledge by teaching adult classes at the fabric store where she works.

MANIPULATIONS

When the fabrics you find aren't quite what you have in mind, consider their potential! Empower yourself with knowledge and experience, and liberate your imagination.

••• MAKING FELT •••

Felt is a nonwoven fabric made from wool fibers. You can design and make your own felt fabric, using precarded and predyed wool, called *roving* or *wool tops.* Carding means that the fibers have been combed so that all are running in the same direction. You will find roving in a variety of colors, from brights to subtle earth tones. It is available in many yarn stores, especially those that sell weaving and spinning supplies. Or it can be purchased through mail-order sources (page 224).

Making felt is a three-stage process, beginning with laying out the fibers in soft, lofty layers. The fibers in each layer must run perpendicular to the layer beneath them, in order for them to interlock and felt together. This is also the stage in which the design of the fabric is determined. The fibers are exposed to water, heat, and pressure in the *felting* stage, causing them to mat together to form a loose fabric. Further agitation and pressure, applied during the *fulling* stage, causes the fabric to shrink and harden into dense, strong felt. The actual process of making felt takes a little "elbow grease," patience, and some readily available supplies. It is fascinating to watch and feel the fibers transforming under your fingers.

The amount of roving required for a project depends not only on the finished size, but also on the desired density. Roughly estimated, 1 ounce (25 g) of roving will produce a 12" × 12" (30.5 × 30.5 cm) square of felt. The best way to determine the amount of roving needed for a project is to make a small test sample first. Take note of the weight of roving used in the sample, the size of the sample before felting, and the amount of shrinkage. Use these findings to estimate the amount of roving needed for a larger project.

Materials

- ◆ Wool roving.
- ◆ Reed mat; placemat, for small projects, window blind or beach mat for larger projects.
- ◆ Soap, such as Ivory Snow® or Murphy's Oil Soap®; mix ¼ cup (50 ml) soap with 1 quart (1 L) hot water.
- ◆ Pitcher, for mixing and pouring soap mixture.
- ◆ Plastic drop cloth.
- ◆ Synthetic screen netting.
- ◆ Wooden dowel, ¾" to 1" (2 to 2.5 cm) thick.
- ◆ Cotton sheeting.
- ◆ Kitchen scale, for measuring ounces of roving.
- ◆ Towels.

■ ■ ■ ■ ■ ■ ■ ■ ■ HOW TO LAY OUT ROVING ■ ■ ■ ■ ■ ■ ■ ■ ■

1 Cover work surface with plastic drop cloth. Place reed mat on drop cloth. Weigh ½ ounce (15 g) roving; divide into three clumps.

2 Pull off small amount from first clump. Tease out fibers into even layer, thin enough to see through; place on mat. Repeat with small amounts, laying out teased pieces of uniform thickness next to each other. Run all fibers in same direction.

4 Lay out third layer, pulling small amounts from last clump. Run all fibers perpendicular to second layer, teasing pieces to uniform thickness.

3 Lay out second layer, pulling small amounts from second clump. Run all fibers perpendicular to first layer, teasing pieces to uniform thickness.

36

■■■■■■■■ HOW TO FELT THE FIBERS ■■■■■■■■

1 Cover roving layers entirely with synthetic screen netting. Sprinkle about 1 cup (250 mL) hot water (as hot as you can stand) over netting. Sprinkle 2 tablespoons (25 mL) soap mixture over netting, near center.

2 Moisten hands with soap mixture. Begin rubbing near center of netting, lightly at first, then applying increasing pressure. Work outward, rubbing entire area.

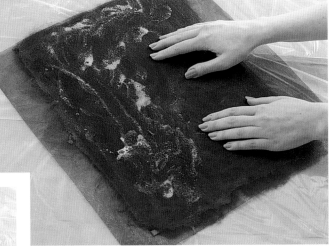

3 Continue rubbing two minutes; gently lift netting from fleece, making sure fibers do not stick to screen. Replace netting; continue rubbing. Add more hot water as needed to keep piece warm. Wipe away excess cool water; piece should be wet but not floating in water. Add soap mixture as needed to keep piece slippery.

4 Continue rubbing. After five minutes, lift netting and begin checking felting progress; pinch a few fibers and lift. If fibers come away from layers, continue felting. If entire piece lifts off mat, move on to fulling stage.

2 Roll the felt and mat together around the wooden dowel.

1 Wipe towel across netting to remove excess soap and water. Remove netting from felt.

3 Roll cotton sheeting around rolled mat. Begin rolling mat back and forth on work surface, applying as much pressure as you can. Felt will shrink in direction it is rolled.

4 Continue rolling and applying pressure. After two minutes, unroll mat; turn felt 90°. Reroll mat and felt together around dowel; roll mat in cotton sheeting. Continue rolling and applying pressure.

5 Repeat step 4 until felt has become hard and will not change shape easily when pulled. Remove fulled felt from mat; rinse out soap under cold running water. Roll up in towel to squeeze out excess moisture.

6 Lay felt on ironing board; cover with press cloth. Press with hot dry iron. This will make the felt smooth and flat with hard surface. Allow to dry thoroughly.

▪ ▪ ▪ ▪ ▪ HOW TO MAKE DESIGNS IN FELT ▪ ▪ ▪ ▪ ▪

Lay out three layers of fibers for background, as in steps 1 to 4 on page 36. Add thin tufts of another color roving for delicate gradation of color. Twist fleece into loose rope to create line of color. Cut shapes from felt colors previously made; lay shapes in design. Add accents, such as wool yarn, silk or rayon threads, or snippets of fabric, covering nonwool items with light layer of wool fibers to adhere them to felt. Felt and full as on pages 37 and 38.

before

after

FELTED WOOL

Felted wools, both woven and knitted, can be used for creative piecing or embellishment. Any wool fabric that has not been treated to resist shrinkage can be felted. Pure wool works best, though you may successfully felt some blends that contain no more than 20% synthetic fibers. Old wool sweaters, especially multicolored and patterned styles, often produce very interesting felted results. Check out the sale tables for wool fabrics; often fabric that is rejected for its color or pattern will take on a more appealing character once it is felted. Experiment with various weave patterns and yarn types, such as bouclés, mohairs, tweeds, and heathers, to produce felted fabrics with various textures and appearances.

Hot water, agitation, and detergent work together to felt the wool. Several garments or pieces of fabric with similar colors can be felted at the same time. Cut away any linings, waistbands, or facings and take down hems, to allow the garment fabric to felt evenly. To prevent sweater sleeves from being stretched, turn them to the inside of the garment or place the sweater in a pillowcase and tie it closed. Placing garments in pillowcases also

traps excess lint. Wash the wool in a full cycle in hot water, using the same amount of detergent you would use for laundering. Repeat the washing until the wool has felted to the desired appearance. It is difficult to distinguish the right from the wrong side of fully felted wool, and grainlines will disappear. However, you may still detect some knit patterns, such as cables and ribbing. Remove the garments from the pillowcases, shake out any excess lint, and tumble dry at a high temperature. The felting process produces a lot of lint, so be sure to clean the lint traps on your washing machine and dryer frequently and tie a nylon stocking over the end of the drain hose.

Press the felted wool from both sides, using a steam iron and a press cloth, and allow the fabric to dry thoroughly before using it. Once felted, the fabric will not ravel, though you may apply a decorative serged edge finish, if desired. Felted wool lends itself naturally to techniques such as raw-edge appliqué (page 43) or butted piecing (opposite). Use a size 90/14 or a 100/16 needle for sewing felted wool.

HOW TO SEW PIECED FELTED WOOL APPLIQUÉS ■ ■ ■ ■

2 Thread machine with rayon embroidery thread. Stitch over butted seams, using decorative machine stitch.

1 Cut felted wool pieces for each section of appliqué. Thread machine with wash-away thread, using regular thread in bobbin. Butt two adjoining pieces; stitch together, using wide zigzag stitch. Repeat for each butted seam.

(continued)

3 Spray appliqué with water to remove wash-away thread. Steam lightly; allow to dry.

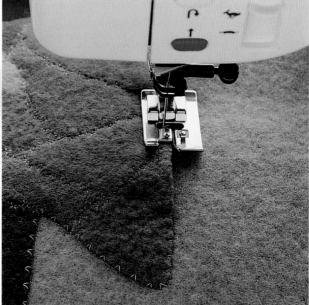

4 Position appliqué on background fabric; pin. Blindstitch around outer edge of appliqué, using invisible thread. (Contrasting thread was used to show detail.)

5 Couch (page 84) decorative cording or yarn over invisible stitching around outer edge of appliqué. Stitch in continuous lines, if possible.

6 Layer appliqués, if desired, for dimensional effect.

EASY RAW-EDGE APPLIQUÉ ON FELTED WOOL ▪▪▪▪▪

1 Cut appliqué shapes; position on background fabric as desired. Secure with glue stick. Stitch ⅛" to ¼" (3 to 6 mm) from edge, using invisible thread.

2 Stitch over stitching line from wrong side of garment, using decorative thread in the bobbin (page 88), or couch (page 84) decorative cording or yarn over stitching line on right side.

▪▪▪▪▪ SEAMS IN FELTED WOOL ▪▪▪▪▪

Lapped seams. Trim seam allowance from one edge; lap over adjoining edge up to seamline. Pin, or secure with basting tape. Topstitch close to edge. Stitch again ¼" (6 mm) from first row of stitching. Trim excess seam allowance on inside of garment.

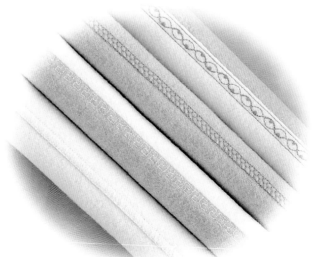

Decorative seams. Follow directions as for lapped seams, stitching seam with one row of decorative machine stitches instead of two straight-stitch rows.

·· PIN WEAVING ··

Pin weaving is a portable weaving method that resembles loom weaving in many ways. In fact, almost any effect you can create with loom weaving can be duplicated in pin weaving. The terms are similar, the techniques are easily adapted, and you don't have to be an experienced weaver or spend a lot of money on equipment to get great results. With pin weaving, fabric can be woven to the exact size and shape of the desired piece, following a pattern outline on the "loom" surface. This allows you to weave accent pieces for garment sections, such as pocket flaps, yokes, lapels, cuffs, and collars. Pillows, table runners, and wall hangings are also suitable projects and provide opportunities for design creativity.

The "loom" in pin weaving consists of pins inserted into a padded, gridded board, to hold the warp yarns. These boards, also used for tasks like pressing quilt blocks and blocking needlework, are available at sewing supply stores, quilt shops, and through mail-order catalogs. If you want to try pin weaving before investing in a padded board, an inexpensive, but effective, version can be made by adhering grid paper to foam-core board.

Depending on the intended location for the pin-woven section and the method by which it will be sewn into the project, you may want to fuse it to lightweight knit interfacing. This is most easily done by applying the interfacing, fusible side up, to the

Warp is the arrangement of strong, usually parallel yarns that establishes the form and provides the strength for the woven piece. In woven fabric, the warp is the lengthwise direction, parallel to the selvages. When using a commercial pattern, you may warp the yarns parallel to the marked lengthwise grainline or perpendicular to it on the crosswise grainline. Or, for creative design purposes, you may wish to establish a new grain direction.

Place warp pins on the seamline to weave fabric to an exact shape with a finished edge. To weave fabric to an exact shape with finished seam allowances, place warp pins on the cutting line, as determined on page 47, step 4. Or place pins 1" to 2" (2.5 to 5 cm) beyond the seamlines to weave oversized fabric that will be cut to shape.

Weft consists of all the elements that are interlaced with the warp, passing over and under it in a systematic way to produce the desired woven design. Weft materials can include decorative yarns, cords and threads, narrow strips of fabric or leather, ribbons, or any other similar material. The weft can be manipulated in any direction except parallel to the warp and can change direction anywhere in the piece.

Weave with continuous weft material, looping over the last warp yarn at each side and returning in the opposite direction, to create selvages. Or weave with the weft material cut 1" to 2" (2.5 to 5 cm) longer than the pattern width to create oversized fabric that will be cut to shape.

Shed is the space formed in the warp to allow easy insertion of the weft material. A narrow stick is woven across the warp in the pattern intended for the weft material. When the stick is turned on edge, it opens the warp, allowing the shuttle, bodkin, or needle room to pass through, carrying the weft material.

Beating is the action of packing or compressing the weft materials to the desired tightness, using a wide-toothed comb, fork, or the fingers. The weft tightness may vary throughout the piece, if desired, creating added design interest. When you pin-weave with ribbons or flat fabric strips, if the desired look is to keep the ribbons or strips flat in their full width, the piece is not beaten.

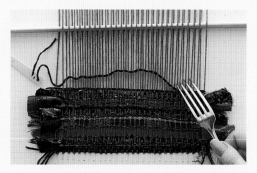

loom surface before pinning the warp. After the piece is woven, it can be fused to the interfacing before removing it from the loom, thus ensuring that its shape will not be altered. This is especially suitable for large pieces loosely woven with weft materials, like ribbons and flat fabric strips. Fusible interfacing is also used anytime you intend to weave an oversized piece and then cut it to a desired shape. However, interfacing is not necessary for smaller pieces that are woven to shape, especially if the weft is fairly tightly compressed or if the piece will be lined.

Pieces can be woven with or without seam allowances, depending on how they will be used. Buttonholes or pocket slits can be created as you weave. Also, since the final shape and all design lines are outlined on the loom surface just under the warp, you can begin weaving in any area desired, perhaps creating strong design interest first, and then filling in unwoven areas later.

Materials

- **Padded, gridded pinning board** or ¼" or ½" (6 mm or 1.3 cm) foam-core board and ¼" or ½" (6 mm or 1.3 cm) grid paper and adhesive.
- **Sturdy straight pins** with small heads.
- **Pin-weaving shuttle** or bodkin, large-eyed blunt needle, or elastic guide.
- **Narrow, flat wooden stick,** for creating a shed.
- **Warp thread,** such as pearl cotton, carpet warp, or cotton yarn.
- **Weft materials,** such as fabric strips, ribbons, yarns, cords, or threads.
- **Beads,** optional.
- **Fine-gauge wire,** for attaching beads to warp cord.
- **Beating tool,** such as wide-toothed comb or fork.

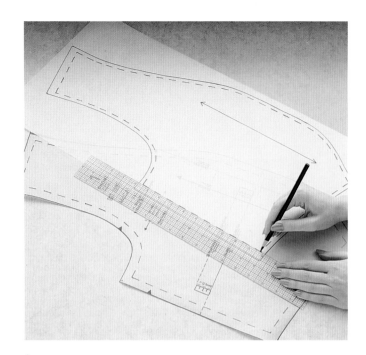

1 Trace pattern seamline onto tracing paper. Trace any darts along stitching lines. Mark any buttonholes or other slits. Mark desired grainline. Draw cutting line ¼" (6 mm) beyond seamline for finished curved edges that will be sewn into a seam or finished edges that will be sewn to lining; draw standard cutting lines on edges that will be cut to size and sewn into garment. Omit step 2 if using purchased pinning board.

2 Adhere grid paper to foam-core board or draw grid directly on board.

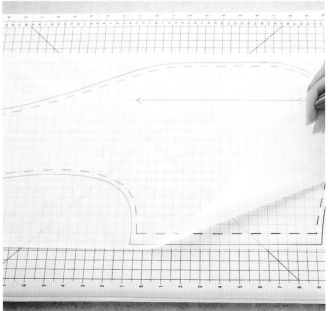

3 Pin prepared pattern faceup on board, aligning desired grainline to grid. If woven piece will be interfaced, preshrink interfacing. Cut interfacing larger than pattern; place fusible side up over pattern.

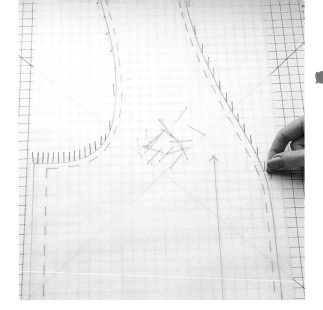

4 Insert warp pins through interfacing and pattern, into board at sharp angle away from pattern. Insert pins along stitching line to create finished edge or along cutting lines, following grid; leave pin heads extending ½" (1.3 cm) from surface. Space pins ¼" to ½" (6 mm to 1.3 cm) apart, depending on the bulkiness of warp yarns and weft materials.

5 Attach warp yarn to corner pin, using slipknot. Keeping even, taut tension, wrap warp yarn back and forth from top to bottom, wrapping around each pin in turn. Secure to last pin with slipknot.

6 Check warp for even tension by running fingers across warp. Tighten any loose warp yarns by moving pin slightly outward.

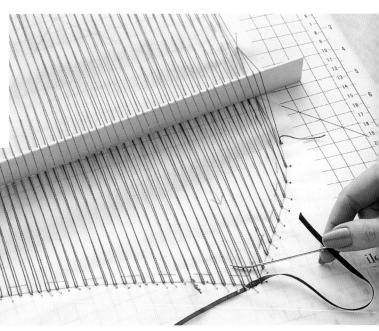

7 Create shed (page 45), weaving it in plain weave pattern (page 49) near center of loom. Turn shed on edge, separating warp yarns.

(continued)

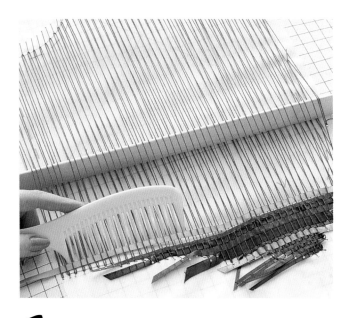

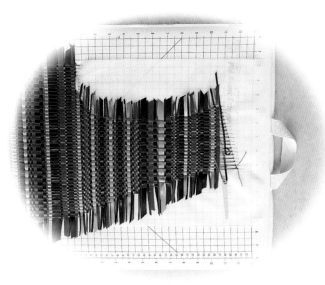

8 Insert weft materials through shed, using shuttle, if desired, and inserting weft in an arc. Beat weft into position against lower warp pins.

9 Weave piece in desired weave patterns (opposite), creating desired design details (pages 50 and 51). Beat weft materials to desired tightness. Complete piece with at least one row of plain weave next to top warp pins. Omit step 10 if piece will not be interfaced.

11 Remove pins. If piece is interfaced, place facedown on pressing surface; press again to completely fuse interfacing. Sew piece into project as desired.

10 Cover woven piece with press cloth; press lightly to partially fuse interfacing to piece.

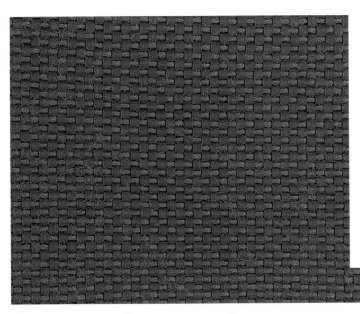

Plain Weave. Pass weft over one warp, under next, over next, continuing in this pattern across row. Reverse the pattern with each succeeding row.

Basket Weave. Pass weft over two warp yarns, under next two, over next two, continuing in this pattern across row. Repeat the pattern with the second row; reverse the pattern with the following two rows. Continue weaving, changing pattern every two rows.

Twill Weave. Pass the weft over two warp yarns, under one, over two, under one, continuing across row. In the second weft row, and each succeeding row, shift the pattern one warp yarn to the right, creating a diagonal pattern.

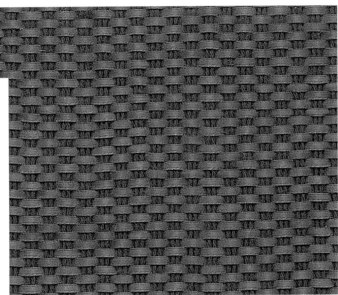

Rib Weave. Pass weft over two warp yarns, under two, over two, under two, continuing in this pattern across row. Reverse the pattern with each succeeding row.

49

WEAVING DESIGN DETAILS

Vertical Slits (a). Plain weave up to the desired slit opening, weaving with separate weft yarns from right and left. Circle the adjacent warp yarns, and weave weft yarns back to their origins, continuing the plain weave. Continue weaving and meeting at same warp yarns until desired slit length is completed. Weave above and below slits with weft yarns that cross entire row.

Horizontal Slits (b). When setting up the warp, insert two additional rows of pins, angled in opposite directions, along marked slit line. String the warp from the top of the project to the top of the slit, and from the bottom of the project to the bottom of the slit. Weave first weft rows above and below slit in plain weave pattern.

Hatching (c) is used to gradually merge one color or type of weft material into another. Start each color on same row on opposite sides of warp. Vary meeting points for several rows, like interlocking fingers, keeping the meetings random, to avoid forming slits. Leave short tails of weft material on back of woven piece.

Dovetailing (d) is similar to hatching, but the meeting warps are planned to create a repeating design.

Stripes. Create horizontal stripes **(e)** by plain weaving several weft rows of solid color, alternated with several contrasting rows. Create vertical stripes **(f)** by alternating weft colors every row in plain weave.

Combining Ribbons and Yarns (g). Create shed in desired weave pattern. Insert ribbons strips to loosely fill lower half of warp, stacking strips one above the other. Remove shed. Weave weft yarns or decorative cords between ribbon strips, in opposite weave pattern from ribbon strips. For added interest, weave weft, using chaining, Soumak, Egyptian knots, or Oriental Soumak (pages 52 and 53).

Free-flowing Designs (h). Insert desired weft materials in various weave patterns and shapes to create strong design lines throughout piece. Weave smaller-scale, varied weft materials around strong design lines, filling in empty spaces. Beat weft materials to desired tightness, varying tightness throughout piece, if desired.

(continued)

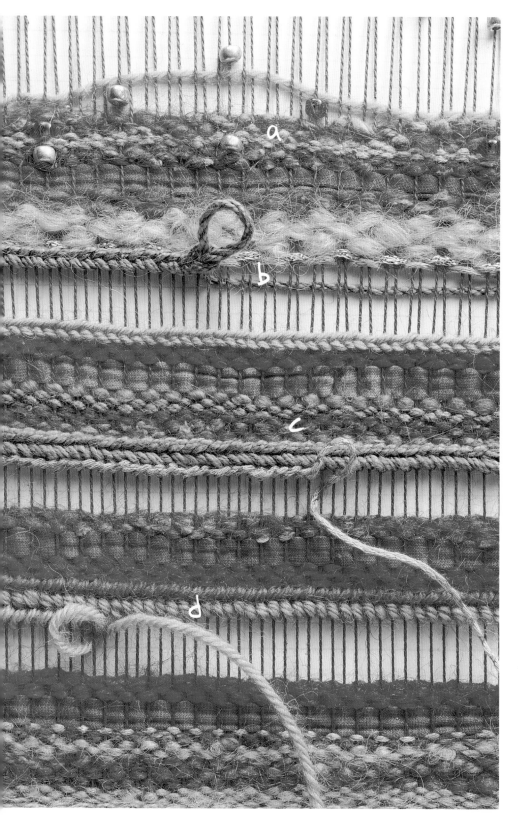

Add beads (a) to warp yarns while stringing the warp, sliding beads to general locations. Work bead into position between weft materials; continue weaving around bead.

Chaining (b) is used to evenly separate and hold warp yarns apart. Run the weft under the warp from right to left. Form a small loop of weft to the left of the first warp yarn; bend it to the right, over the first warp. Reach through this loop and pull up a new loop of weft from under the warp. Bend new loop over to the right; tighten first loop. Continue across warp, chaining over each warp yarn in turn. After chaining over last warp yarn, pull weft through remaining loop to secure.

Soumak (c) is a technique of wrapping the weft around the warp to create textural interest. Draw the weft over the top of the first warp, down around it, then over it and the next warp, continuing across the warp in this forward over two, back under one pattern. After beating, the soumak forms a series of slightly sloping lines. By changing the direction of the slope on alternate wefts, you can create a herringbone or chevron pattern.

Egyptian knot (d) is an upside-down Soumak; work the weft forward under two warps and then back over one warp, and repeat across.

Oriental Soumak (e) is similar to Soumak. The weft is taken over four warps, back under two, forward over four, back under two, and so on.

Cavandoli knot (f) is made with the weft forming two half-hitch knots, one above the other, on one warp thread.

Greek knot (g) is a series of three half-hitches made one above the other on one warp yarn. Repeat it across as many warp yarns as desired to build a honeycomb of texture or use it alone for interest. Surround it with plain weave to make it more apparent.

Lark's head knot (h) is worked with individually cut yarns or fabric strips. Wrap the yarn under two warp yarns and then draw a loop of it up between the warps. Insert the ends through the loop and draw tight. When applying a series of lark's head knots, leave ends at random lengths for more interest.

RANDOM-CUT FABRIC WEAVING

Fabric artists often create "new cloth" from a collection of coordinating fabrics that are cut and pieced together. One method for creating this new cloth is called fabric weaving, in which fabric strips are interwoven and applied to a foundation. For visual interest, the strips are often cut with gently curving edges in varying widths. Random-cut fabric weaving allows you to use a variety of fabrics in both the warp and the weft, producing a new cloth with multiple colors, patterns, and visual textures.

The woven fabric strips are attached to a foundation of either fusible knit interfacing or a lightweight flannel. The raw edges of the strips, characteristic of fabric weaving, may be lightly secured with machine-guided or free-motion (page 181) stitching; additional decorative stitching may be used to create visual texture. Select fusible interfacing for the foundation if the intended purpose of the fabric is for a lightweight garment with a small amount of decorative stitching. If the fabric will be used for a heavier garment or if you intend to incorporate a lot of decorative stitching, select a flannel foundation.

Because garment pieces will be cut from your newly woven cloth, weave sections that are just large enough for each piece. Use a padded pinning board for your weaving surface; prepare small pieces on an ironing board. For ease of explanation in the directions that follow, the warp strips are cut beginning with the far left strip and working toward the right; the weft strips are cut from the top strip to the bottom strip. You may reverse the order or work from the center outward once you understand the technique.

Materials

- Lightweight fabrics, in a variety of coordinating colors and prints; avoid fabrics that will ravel excessively.
- Rotary cutter and cutting mat.
- Padded pinning board, or foam-core board; pins.
- Fusible knit interfacing for foundation, if fabric will be used for lightweight garment with minimal decorative stitching.
- Lightweight cotton flannel for foundation, if woven fabric will be used for heavier garment or be heavily stitched.
- Masking tape, optional.

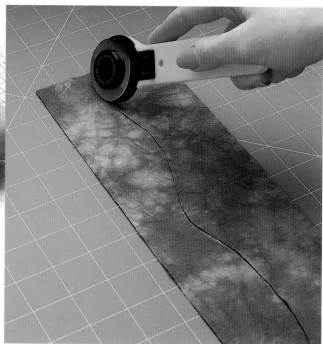

1 Cut a piece of desired foundation material slightly larger than dimensions of the pattern piece; smooth onto surface of pinning board. If using fusible knit interfacing, apply to the pinning board fusible side up. Secure foundation to board, pinning or taping around outer edges.

2 Sketch weave pattern, if desired, roughly planning size, shape, and number of strips necessary. Cut far left warp strip in desired width, length, and shape, using rotary cutter and mat.

3 Lap long right edge of first strip over second fabric. Cut second strip, using right edge of first strip as cutting guide for left edge and cutting right edge as desired.

4 Place first strip in position over foundation on pinning board; pin. Lap long right edge of second strip over third fabric. Cut third strip, using right edge of second strip as cutting guide for left edge and cutting right edge as desired.

5 Cut each warp strip, using previous strip as cutting guide for left edge. Pin each strip in position over foundation after using it as cutting guide.

6 Cut weft strips, beginning with top strip and working toward bottom. Use lower edge of previous strip as cutting guide for upper edge of each strip. Weave weft strips through warp strips, aligning edges snugly while keeping strips flat; pin in position.

(continued)

■ ■ ■ HOW TO WEAVE RANDOM-CUT FABRIC STRIPS (continued)

7 **Fusible interfacing foundation.** Cover woven piece with press cloth; press lightly to partially fuse interfacing to piece. Remove woven piece from surface. Place facedown on pressing surface; press again to completely fuse interfacing.

7 **Flannel foundation.** Pin strips to foundation around outer edge and throughout piece. Remove woven piece from surface. Baste around outer edge. Stitch each strip to foundation, beginning with center strips of warp and weft, and working outward. Stitch near outer edges on both sides of strips, or stitch wandering lines through center of strips.

8 Add machine-guided or free-motion decorative stitches as desired.

Cut all warp strips from the same print fabric. Select progressively lighter colors for the weft strips, beginning with dark strips at the top.

Cut strips more narrow through the center of the piece, widening them toward the outer edges.

Experiment with different weave patterns, such as this basket weave (over two, under one).

QUILTED EFFECTS ▪▪▪▪▪▪

Many fabric artists include some form of quilting in their projects, whether these are made from pieced fabric or whole cloth. Quilting adds wonderful texture and dimension, a feast for the eyes as well as the fingertips. Decorative threads, double-needle stitching (page 91), and even decorative bobbin thread sewing (page 88) may be used for special effects. The challenge in successful apparel quilting is to acquire the desired appearance without forfeiting the drapable quality of the fabric. Ideally, a quilted garment is comfortable and soft, molding to the body's form rather than holding a stiff shape of its own. The fabrics and battings selected as well as the density and style of quilting stitches all affect the final appearance and drape of the garment.

Quilting Basics

The possibilities for quilted effects are seemingly endless. Some techniques are machine-guided, meaning the feed dogs and presser foot guide the fabric. An Even Feed® foot is useful for feeding fabric and batting layers evenly to prevent puckers, though for some intricate work, an open-toe embroidery foot allows better visibility. While machine-guided quilting is helpful for some effects, such as marked gridwork **(a),** you may find it cumbersome and limiting for effects like echo quilting **(b)** or small-scale background quilting **(c),** techniques that require frequent directional changes. In free-motion quilting, the layers are guided by hand, allowing you to stitch in any direction without turning the fabric and to stitch tight corners and intricate curves with ease.

Garment quilting often consists of repetitive lines or designs filling in areas for backgound texture. Many geometric quilting patterns (left) used by fabric artists are based on the Japanese Sashiko style of quilting, in which a gridwork of repetitive designs is completed by stitching in a continuous line, following an efficient, predetermined path. Try some of the examples shown here or on pages 64 and 65, or work out unique patterns of your own on graph paper, charting efficient stitch paths. Mark the pattern on your fabric, and stitch the designs in either machine-guided or free-motion quilting.

Whenever possible, complete the quilting before cutting garment pieces to size, as the quilting process will shrink the size of the fabric. This also gives you excess fabric to grasp when you are doing free-motion quilting. For garments with shoulder seams, cut the front and back pieces with generous seam and hem allowances on all but the shoulder seam. Join the pieces at the shoulder before layering and quilting, minimizing bulk and allowing you to quilt in a continuous pattern from the front to the back.

Batting

One of the keys to creating drapable quilted fabric is selecting the appropriate batting. Many low-loft and extra-low-loft battings are available, including those with fiber contents of cotton, polyester, cotton/polyester blend, and wool. Each of these fibers has characteristics that determine the batting's suitability for your project. Cotton battings are very soft, drapable, and breathable for lightweight garments. They may tend to separate or bunch easily and must therefore be quilted with no more than 2" to 3" (5 to 7.5 cm) spaces between stitches. Polyester is more stable, so the quilting lines can be farther apart, but fiber ends may tend to *beard,* or penetrate through to the surface of the fabric. Blended battings take advantage of the positive characteristics of both fibers. Wool batting is soft, warm, and resilient, and has firmer body than cotton or polyester. *Needlepunching* is a process that gives the batting firmer body to resist separation or bunching, allowing you to quilt with larger spaces between stitching lines. While this is desirable for larger quilts and crafting or home decorating projects, it may be too firm for a garment. For shrinkage control,

natural-fiber battings should be prewashed, following the manufacturer's directions. However, some artists prefer to quilt the fabric with unwashed batting and then wash and dry the quilted piece before cutting out garment sections. This produces a deeper "dimpling" of the surface. For a thinner look, batting may also be split in half, though if you intend to prewash the batting, split it after washing and drying. Cotton flannel fabric is another useful alternative to batting when a thin appearance is desired. Due to its high rate of shrinkage, cotton flannel should always be prewashed.

Fabric

The fabric selected will naturally play a major role in the final drapability and appearance of the quilted garment. Lightweight to mediumweight closely woven natural-fiber fabrics produce the best results, with softly dimpled texture. Fine-quality pure cotton fabric is easiest to work with and the most widely used. Silk fabrics, including broadcloth, noile, dupioni, and crepe-de-chine produce luxurious quilted effects. Frequent needle changes may be necessary for extensive sewing on silk because the filament may dull the needle and

Experiment with various battings, fabrics, yarns, and threads to develop a combination with your preferred drapability, texture, and artistic appeal.

cause skipped stitches. Rayon is soft and drapes well, but like some silks, it is slippery and shifts easily during construction. Linen is characteristically crisp; you may want to wash and dry it several times for a softer quilted look. Washing any fabric before quilting will help to eliminate skipped stitches.

Select lightweight backing fabric with the same qualities as the outer fabric, especially if the project is intended to be reversible. If your outer fabric is a solid color, consider using a print backing fabric and motif-quilting from the backing side, thus "sketching" the print onto the outer fabric in quilting stitches.

Threads

Select threads according to the effect you want to create. Invisible nylon thread works well when quilted background texture is your goal. It is also useful when quilting multicolored or pieced fabric, as it blends easily from one color to the next. Select cotton or polyester thread in a color to match or coordinate with the fabric when you want the quilting stitches to be more visible, yet subtle. Decorative threads draw attention, making them the primary focus over the quilted texture. Rayon and cotton emboidery threads and some metallic threads can be threaded through the machine needle and sewn on the right side. Though some heavier decorative threads will fit through the eye of a larger needle, consider sewing with the decorative thread in the bobbin (page 88). This allows you to use a smaller machine needle, resulting in better quality quilting stitches. Couching (page 84) is another technique that can be used to simultaneously quilt and embellish the fabric.

Always make a test sample, 12" to 15" (30.5 to 38 cm) square, using the desired batting, outer fabric, and backing fabric. Divide the sample into sections, quilting areas with varying densities and stitch styles. This is a good time to try some new techniques, such as couching or decorative bobbin thread stitching, or to practice free-motion sewing skills. Measure your sample after quilting; then wash and dry it. Measure it again, and evaluate the piece for loft, size, texture or smoothness, drapability or stiffness, and the condition of the batting in unstitched areas.

■ ■ ■ HOW TO PREPARE FABRIC FOR QUILTING ■ ■ ■

2 Place backing fabric facedown on work surface; place batting over backing fabric. Place garment fabric faceup over batting. Baste layers together, using grid of hand basting or safety pins, spaced about 3" (7.5 cm) apart. Closer basting lines may be necessary if fabric is slippery or if you will not be using an Even Feed® presser foot.

1 Preshrink outer fabric and backing fabric, if necessary. Wash and dry batting, if desired, following manufacturer's directions. Split batting, if desired. Mark design or guidelines (page 214) on right side of outer fabric if quilting will be done from outside; mark on right side of backing fabric if quilting will be done from backing side.

TIPS FOR MACHINE-GUIDED QUILTING

Attach Even Feed® presser foot or walking foot for strip quilting **(a)** or straight-line stitching. Set machine for a straight stitch with 10 to 12 stitches per inch (2.5 cm).

Attach open-toe embroidery foot for intricate machine-guided quilting stitches that require more visibility **(b)**.

Position hands on either side of presser foot. Gently press down and hold fabric taut to prevent layers from shifting, causing puckers or tucks. Ease any excess fabric under the presser foot as you stitch.

Begin and end stitching lines with 8 to 10 very short stitches to secure threads.

Stitch-in-the-ditch quilting. Stitch over seamlines in pieced fabric, stitching in the well of the seams.

Channel quilting. Stitch a series of relatively parallel lines. To create more interest, lines need not be evenly spaced.

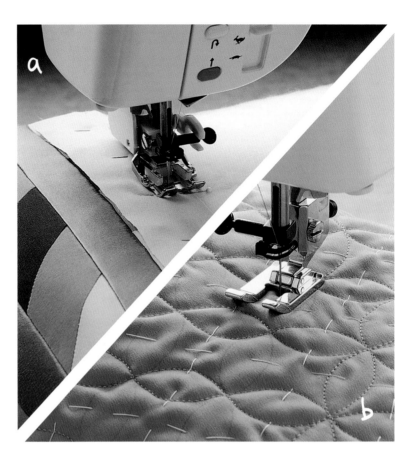

IDEAS FOR MACHINE-GUIDED BACKGROUND QUILTING

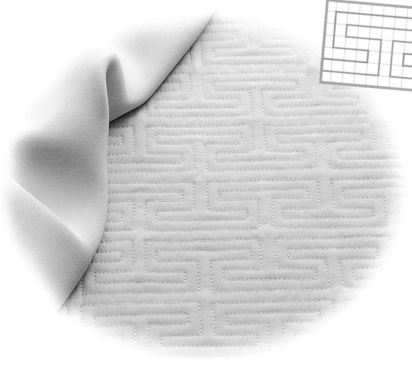

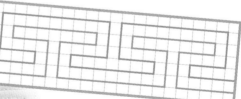

First stitch the green lines throughout the entire piece. Then stitch the pink lines.

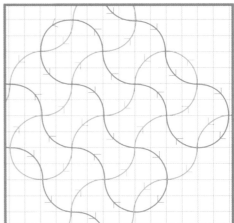

First stitch lines shown in green throughout entire piece. Then stitch lines shown in pink, stitching across previous stitches.

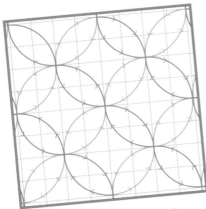

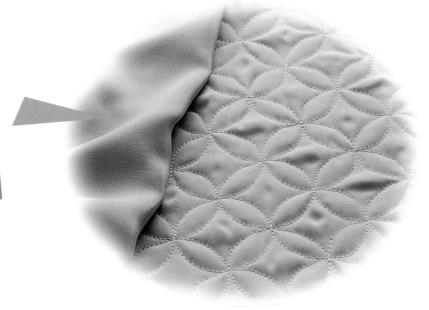

Stitch a continuous wavy pass across entire piece and back, as shown in green. Repeat for each green set. Then stitch all pink lines across and back.

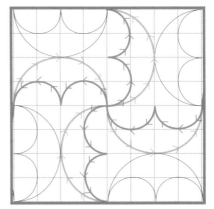

Stitch wide arcs throughout entire piece, as indicated in green. Then stitch all narrower arcs, as indicated in pink.

Set machine for straight stitch. Attach darning foot. Lower or cover feed dogs. If neither option is possible with your machine, set stitch length at 0.

Lower the presser foot. This is not always obvious when using a darning foot.

Position hands so they act as a hoop, encircling needle. Gently press down and pull outward to create tension on fabric. Move fabric with wrist and hand movements as you stitch. Rest elbows comfortably on sewing table while stitching; it may be helpful to elevate elbows on books. Wear rubber fingertip covers for more control.

Begin and end stitching lines with 8 to 10 very short stitches to secure threads.

Maintain steady rhythm and speed as you stitch to keep the stitch length uniform.

Motif quilting. Outline desired motifs in a print; stitch from one motif to another with continuous stitches.

Marked-design quilting. Outline design first. Then stitch inner design lines, moving continuously from one area to another.

Echo quilting. Outline a central motif or design. Stitch evenly spaced lines, moving outward from the motif or design.

Continuous-line background quilting. Any pattern that can be drawn on paper without lifting the pencil can also be stitched without stopping. These lines are often stitched around a motif, appliqué, or trapunto design to make it more apparent.

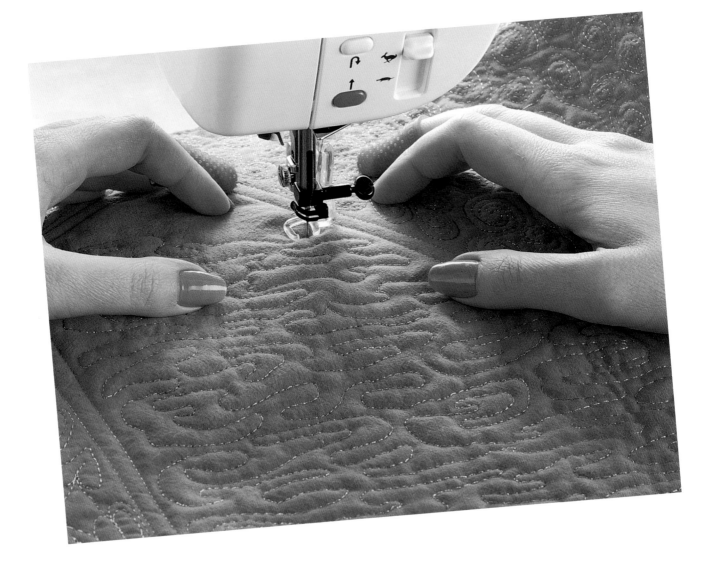

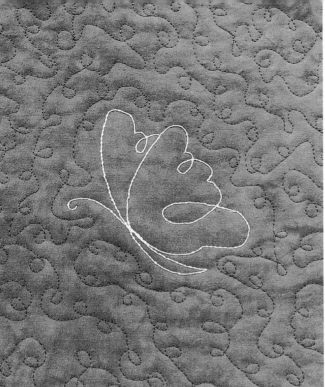

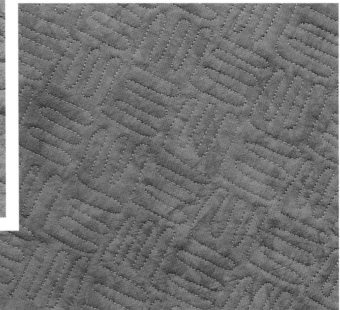

Curvy lines and loops of the butterfly motif are repeated continuously in the background quilting.

Alternating parallel stitching lines fill an area with a square grid design.

Wavy lines resemble rippling water.

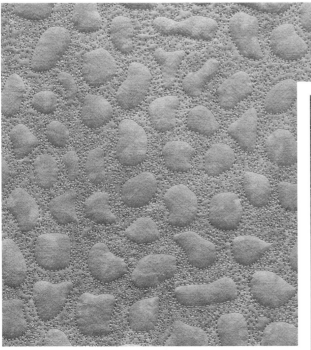

Outlined shapes become more pronounced when separated with stippling stitches.

... TRAPUNTO ...

Trapunto, also known as *Italian quilting*, is a versatile quilting technique that raises the elements of a design for a three-dimensional effect. Traditionally, design shapes were outlined in hand stitching through two layers of fabric. Tiny slits were then cut into the backing fabric and stuffing was inserted through the holes to pad the shapes. Trapunto adapts well to machine sewing, which speeds up the process and produces impressive results. Using this method, shapes are padded with batting as they are stitched, a technique made easier by innovative sewing notions, like wash-away thread and water-soluble marking pens. Because the fabric must be wetted to remove wash-away thread and marking pen, this method for padded designs is only suitable for washable fabric or fabric that will not be damaged by spraying it with water.

Corded quilting is another style of trapunto in which narrow stitched channels are filled with yarn to create ridges. This makes a subtle, but effective, accent along front opening edges or hems. Padded designs and corded quilting work well together or can be used alone. Additional quilting (page 60) can be worked between corded quilting rows or around padded designs to enhance them.

The shadows and highlights of trapunto's dimensional effects are more apparent when worked on solid-color fabrics. Finely woven natural-fiber fabrics, including cotton, wool, and silk, work well. Linen can be softened first by washing and tumbling dry. Synthetic fabrics may tend to pucker around the padded areas more than natural fabrics. Prints tend to obscure the design, and your work will be in vain. However, trapunto can be used to emphasize and give dimension to a portion of a print, such as a distinct floral motif. Any method of trapunto will alter the size of the fabric, so it is important to preshrink the fabric and complete the trapunto before cutting out pattern pieces.

Work a test sample to determine the machine settings for free-motion stitching, the width of stitched channels, and the number of yarn strands necessary for corded quilting. Underfilled channels are not as visually effective; overfilled channels may produce puckers or stiffness.

Materials

- ◆ Outer fabric.
- ◆ Backing fabric.
- ◆ Lightweight fusible interfacing, optional.
- ◆ High-loft batting; low-loft batting.
- ◆ Acrylic baby yarn and yarn needle.
- ◆ Wash-away thread.
- ◆ Fabric marker.
- ◆ Stylus.

2 Thread machine with wash-away thread; use regular sewing thread in the bobbin. Attach presser foot, and adjust machine for desired technique. Stitch on outer design lines.

1 Transfer design (page 214) to right side of outer fabric. Pin high-loft batting to wrong side of fabric; baste or secure with safety pins.

3 Trim away batting in areas that are to appear flat, using blunt-end scissors and trimming close to stitching line.

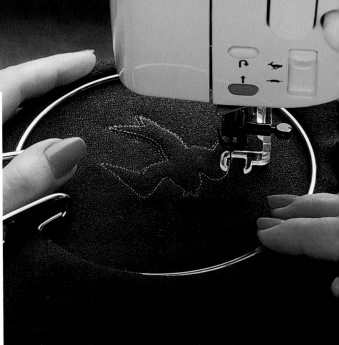

4 Layer outer fabric over lightweight batting and backing fabric; pin-baste or hand-baste layers together.

5 Thread machine with regular sewing thread or decorative thread. Stitch around design, stitching close to previous stitches; stitch any interior design lines. Fill in flat areas around padded design with quilting stitches (page 60), if desired.

6 Spray nonwashable quilted fabric **(a)** with cool water to remove wash-away thread. Or immerse washable quilted fabric **(b)** in cool water one to two minutes to dissolve wash-away thread and remove water-soluble marker lines, if used. Dry flat, or tumble dry to create more texture.

HOW TO SEW CORDED QUILTING

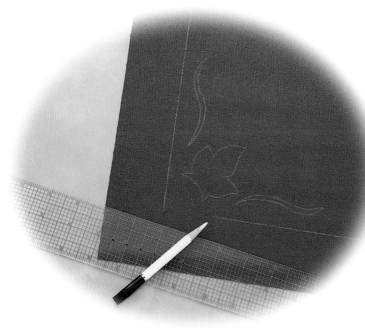

1 Preshrink outer fabric, backing fabric, and any interfacing. Apply interfacing, if desired, following manufacturer's directions. Transfer design (page 214) to right side of fabric. For continuous rows, mark first row; use presser foot as guide for additional rows.

2 Pin outer fabric to backing fabric, wrong sides together; baste. Stitch design lines, using embroidery foot or Even Feed® foot.

3 Thread yarn needle with several strands of yarn (number determined in test sample) cut to full length of channel. Insert yarn into channel.

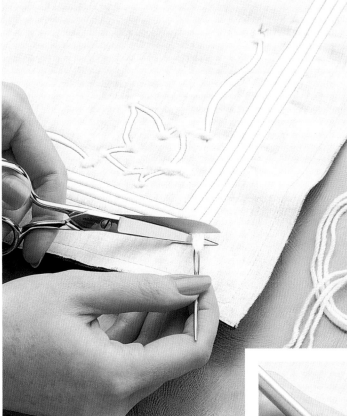

4 Bring needle through backing fabric at corner; trim yarn.

5 Repeat steps 3 and 4, filling all channels. Poke yarn ends under backing fabric, using stylus. Place completed fabric facedown on padded pressing surface; press lightly.

Shallow pleats add textural interest to your sewing project. They can be used for cuffs, collars, pockets, or inserts on garments. Pillows, placemats, and cornice boards may be enhanced with pleated fabric. A cloth pleater, designed for making perfectly spaced pleats, allows you to pleat the fabric before cutting your pattern, and eliminates the need for tedious marking and basting. By skipping slots in the pleater, you can vary the size and spacing of the pleats. The pleats can be held in place permanently with fusible interfacing, decorative topstitching, or couching, if desired.

Many fabrics are suitable for pleated effects. Best results are achieved with lightweight to mediumweight fabrics. Depending on the pleat design, the process may require fabric two to three times the size of the finished piece. Pleats made in 100% polyester fabric can be permanently set by using a press cloth and an iron set at a high temperature. This is especially suitable for edgings and any other pleated accents that are not held in place by decorative stitching or fusing.

PLEATED EFFECTS

Use of the pleater does not limit you to perfect, evenly spaced pleats. Many interesting variations can be developed. Experiment with irregular pleating and even create erratic, free-form effects. Change the grainline in any direction you choose. Turn pleats in opposite directions from each other. Create irregular folds or run a crosswise fold through the fabric before pleating. Once you begin to experiment, you will find there are no restrictions to your pleating creativity.

Materials

- ◆ Cloth pleater, such as EZE Pleater™ or Perfect Pleater™.
- ◆ Lightweight to mediumweight fabric.
- ◆ Lightweight fusible interfacing.
- ◆ Decorative thread for topstitching or couching.

HOW TO USE A CLOTH PLEATER ■ ■ ■ ■ ■ ■ ■ ■ ■ ■ ■ ■ ■ ■ ■ ■

1 Position pleater on pressing surface with folds facing away from you. Place fabric facedown over pleater, allowing edge nearest you to extend at least ⅝" (1.5 cm) off pleater, for seam allowance.

2 Tuck fabric behind cloth-covered louver, using fingers or point turner. Repeat until three or four pleats have been formed. Press with steam iron.

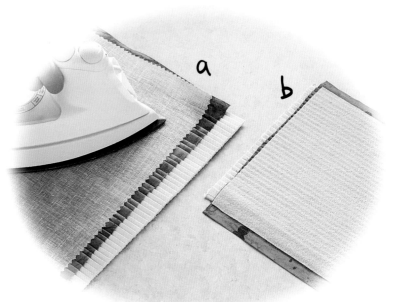

3 Repeat step 2 until desired length has been pleated. Allow enough excess unpleated fabric for seaming.

4 Cover pleated fabric with damp press cloth; set iron at high temperature. Press entire piece until press cloth is dry, to set pleats **(a).** Or place fusible interfacing, fusible side down, over pleated fabric; fuse, following manufacturer's directions, to lock pleats **(b).**

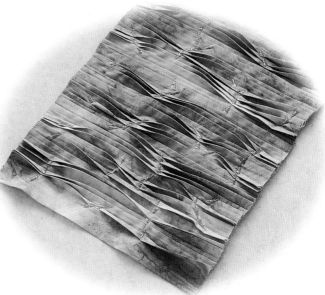

5 Allow fabric to cool. Roll pleater back to release fabric. Place pleated fabric, right side up, on pressing surface; press again to sharpen folds.

6 Embellish pleated fabric with decorative machine stitching or couching, if desired.

HOW TO JOIN PLEATED PANELS

1 Lap one panel over the next so pleats form continuous pattern. Pin folded edge of lapped pleat through all layers.

2 Turn pinned fabric facedown; pin seam allowances together. Stitch and finish.

77

TEXTURIZING FABRICS ■ ■ ■ ■ ■ ■ ■

Smooth fabrics can be texturized to give them more visual and tactile appeal. Sections of texturized fabric can be incorporated into a pieced cloth to create an interesting wall hanging or pillow front. Or they can become an intriguing design element in an artistic garment.

Some methods of texturizing, such as bubbling and crinkling, require that you first manipulate the fabric in some way to create the texture. The texture is then permanently retained by fusing interfacing to the wrong side of the fabric.

To texturize by shrinking, select two natural fabrics that will shrink when they are washed but will not be damaged by hot water. Cotton, linen, rayon, and some silks will work well for the outer fabric. If the foundation fabric will show, you can use the same or similar fabric; otherwise, simple cotton muslin will work. The outer fabric is preshrunk; the foundation fabric is not. Once the two fabrics are sewn together, washing and drying them causes the foundation to shrink, thus puckering the outer fabric.

Consider the final use for the texturized fabric when you are preparing it. It is easier to work with small pieces rather than one large one, if your project will permit.

■ ■ ■ ■ ■ ■ ■ HOW TO BUBBLE FABRIC ■ ■ ■ ■ ■ ■

Materials

◆ Fabric.
◆ Raised metal grid, such as kitchen cooling rack; pencil with rubber eraser.
◆ Lightweight fusible knit interfacing.

1 Cut 18" (46 cm) square of fabric. Wet fabric thoroughly; squeeze out excess moisture. Place damp fabric, right side down, over slightly raised metal grid, such as kitchen cooling rack.

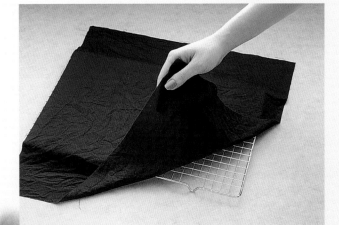

2 Poke fabric down ½" (1.3 cm) into each hole of grid, using eraser end of pencil; begin at center and work outward, controlling fabric with fingers. Fabric will shrink up to about half its size.

(continued)

3 Cut fusible interfacing to same size as bubbled fabric; place, fusible side down, over bubbled fabric. Press interfacing to fuse while fabric is still in grid. Allow fabric to dry thoroughly.

4 Gently remove fabric from grid. Embellish with decorative stitching, if desired.

HOW TO CRINKLE FABRIC

Materials

- Fabric, preferably natural.
- Cotton string or thick rubber bands; hosiery.
- Washer and dryer.
- Lightweight fusible interfacing.

1 Wet fabric thoroughly in lukewarm water; squeeze out excess moisture. Place fabric flat on work surface. Gather fabric with fingers along lengthwise grain, forming narrow roll.

2 Twist ends of roll in opposite directions, squeezing out any bubbles that form while twisting; continue twisting until fabric is twisted as tight as possible and begins to curl.

3 Fold twisted roll in half, if necessary. Continue twisting, allowing fabric to curl into small, twisted ball.

4 Tie ball with cotton string or secure with thick rubber bands. Tie ball into toe of hosiery. Dry fabric in clothes dryer with towels; towels absorb moisture and help reduce noise. Depending on amount of fabric, this step could take several hours.

(continued)

5 Unroll dry fabric gently; place, right side down, on pressing surface. Spread fabric to desired width, smoothing crinkles to desired texture.

6 Place fusible interfacing, fusible side down, over crinkled fabric. Fuse interfacing, following manufacturer's directions.

Materials

♦ Natural fabric, such as cotton, linen, rayon, or silk, for outer fabric.

♦ Untreated natural fabric, such as 78/76 muslin or cotton flannel, for foundation fabric.

♦ Washer and dryer.

1 Wash outer fabric in warm water; machine dry. Press. Do not preshrink foundation fabric. Place outer fabric over foundation fabric, wrong sides together; pin around outer edges and throughout interior.

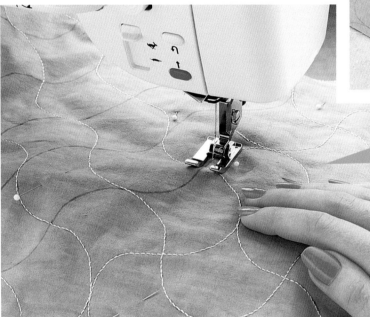

2 Stitch fabric to foundation, following desired grid pattern, such as squares or diamonds. Stitching lines may be wavy or straight; spaces between lines should be no more than 1½" to 2" (3.8 to 5 cm) wide.

3 Wash stitched fabric in very hot water; machine dry. Foundation fabric will shrink, causing outer fabric to ripple and pucker.

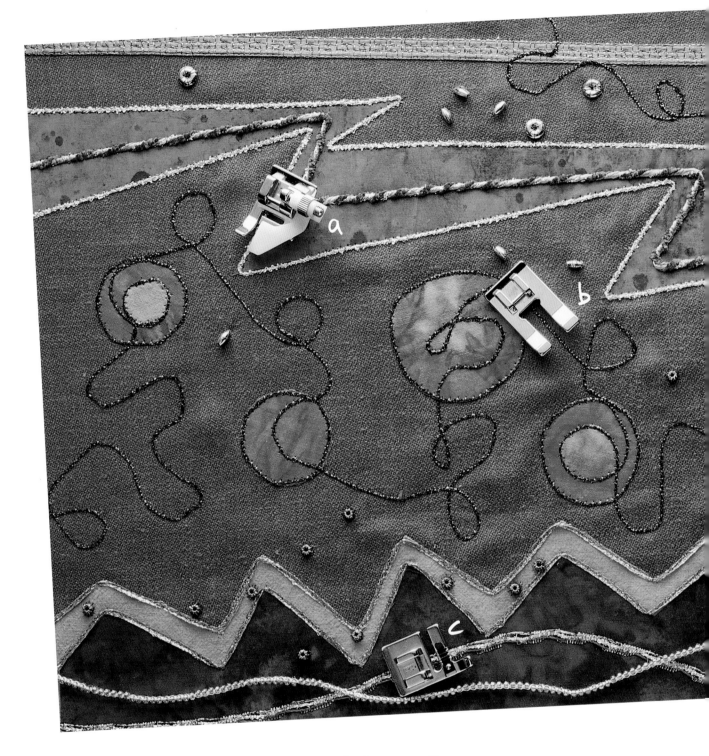

COUCHING

Apply decorative cords, yarns, and ribbons to the fabric surface by couching. Arrange the trim on the fabric surface, following marked design lines, and stitch over it, using one of several stitch options. Use monofilament thread and a blindstitch or simple zigzag pattern for nearly invisible stitches, allowing the decorative cords to seemingly float on the surface of the fabric. If you want to incorporate the machine

thread into the overall effect, use regular sewing thread or decorative thread in the desired color and stitch over the trim, using a zigzag, multiple zigzag, or decorative stitch pattern. Experiment with various decorative stitches to get the look you want. Some flat trims and ribbons can be couched onto the surface, using a double needle (page 91) and a decorative machine stitch.

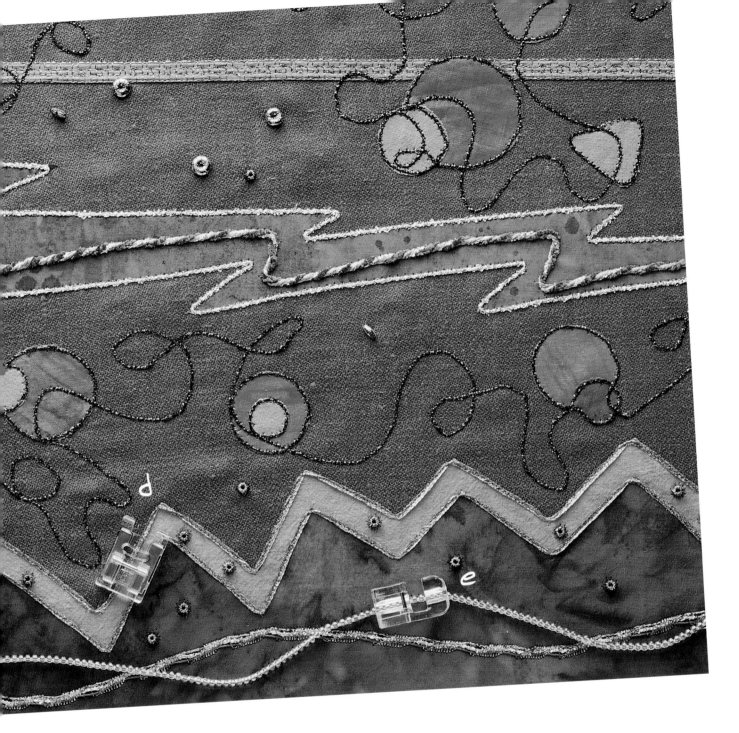

Presser feet suitable for couching feature recessed bottoms or guides for feeding the trims. These include a blind hem foot (a), an Open-toe embroidery foot (b), a cording foot (c), a buttonhole foot (d), and a Pearls 'n Piping™ foot (e).

Couch trims ¼" (6 mm) or narrower, using an open-toe embroidery foot. Apply very small trims with a cording foot, freeing your hands to guide the fabric while the foot guides the trim. A blind hem foot or other specialty presser foot may also be used. Stabilize (page 218) lightweight or mediumweight fabric with fusible interfacing or removable stabilizer. It is usually not necessary to stabilize heavy fabrics or quilted fabrics.

Whenever possible, cut the decorative trim to the desired length plus additional length for finishing. Couching trims directly off a spool or skein creates extra tension and may cause puckering. As with any other technique, it is important to practice on a sample of the fabric to determine stitch settings and the easiest method for guiding the trim.

1 Attach desired presser foot to machine. Thread machine with desired sewing thread or decorative thread; wind bobbin with lightweight thread. Apply stabilizer under fabric, if desired. Cut trim to desired length plus 8" to 10" (20.5 to 25.5 cm). Insert trim through hole in presser foot or position trim under foot with 4" (10 cm) excess behind foot.

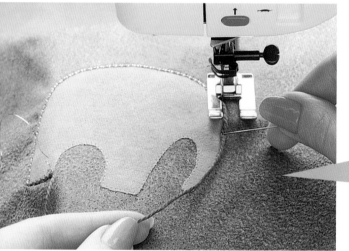

2 Adjust stitch width so stitches catch fabric on both sides of trim, if using zigzag or blind hem stitch. Set stitch length at about 10 stitches per inch (2.5 cm). Or set stitches as determined in practice sample. Stitch, guiding fabric to follow design and allowing trim to feed freely. Guide trim with hand needle in intricate areas.

3 Ease trim around curves. Turn sharp corners with needle down in fabric on same side of trim as direction of turn.

4 Secure threads at beginning and end of stitching line by pulling to back side and knotting. Secure ends of couched trim as shown opposite. Remove stabilizer and markings as necessary. Press lightly from back side, taking care not to flatten trim.

FINISH ENDS OF COUCHED TRIMS ▪ ▪ ▪ ▪ ▪

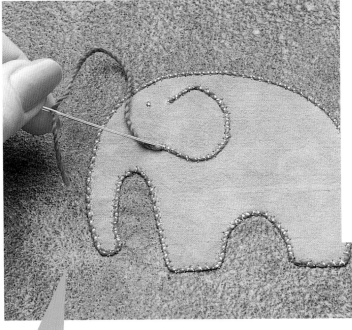

Apply liquid fray preventer to wide trim at end of stitching line; allow to dry. Trim even with end of stitching line.

Thread end of narrow cord or yarn through tapestry needle, and stitch to wrong side; knot together with bobbin and top threads on wrong side. Clip trim, leaving short tail.

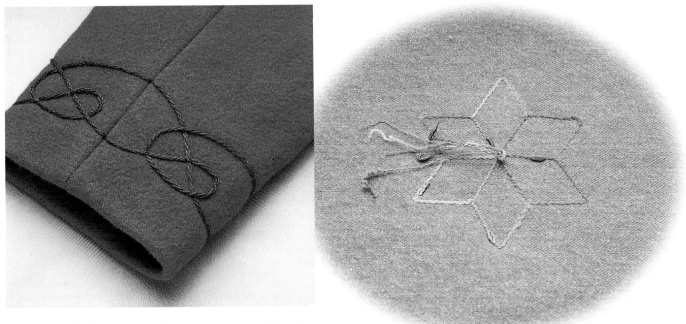

Enclose end of trim in seamline whenever possible. Or cover end with appliqué.

Knot multiple cord ends together at end of stitching line; allow to fray or hang freely for decorative effect.

DECORATIVE BOBBIN THREAD SEWING ▪ ▪ ▪ ▪ ▪ ▪ ▪ ▪ ▪ ▪ ▪

Decorative threads too thick to thread through the eye of the sewing machine needle can be wound on the bobbin and stitched onto the surface from the wrong side of the fabric. Because the stitching is done facedown, even the artist must wait to view the results. Exquisite designs can be created using metallic threads, pearl cotton, pearl rayon, ribbon threads, or embroidery floss. The stitching may follow a marked design **(a),** using machine-guided stitching or using free-motion techniques. For a free-form effect, areas can be stitched with free-motion random stippling **(b)** or decorated more heavily with free-motion fill-in stitches **(c).** Rows of decorative stitch

patterns or utility stitch patterns **(d)** can be used to create attractive edgings or borders.

Experimentation is the key to success in decorative bobbin thread stitching. A few basic guidelines and a little practice will help you eliminate the guesswork in achieving the look you want. Begin experimenting with straight stitches. Generally, the character of the decorative threads and cords is better defined when the machine stitch length is set at eight to ten stitches per inch (2.5 cm). Enlarge decorative stitch patterns and utility stitch patterns whenever possible for a more pronounced look. Try various threads and cords in your bobbin to see which ones produce the desired results. Follow your sewing machine manufacturer's instructions for adjusting or bypassing bobbin thread tension. Thread the sewing machine needle with invisible nylon thread or regular sewing thread in a color to match the background fabric. Adjust needle thread tension, if necessary, to produce the desired quality of stitches on the decorative side.

Wind decorative threads onto wind-in-place bobbins by hand, using firm, even tension and winding in the same direction as the bobbin would be wound on the machine. Wind other bobbins on the machine at slow speed, bypassing tension discs. Hold a large or awkward spool on a pencil or place it in a jar on the floor, controlling thread tension with the fingers.

TIPS FOR SEWING WITH DECORATIVE BOBBIN THREAD

Mark design guidelines on stabilizer; for asymmetrical designs, mark mirror image. Press freezer paper, shiny side down, to wrong side of fabric. Or baste tear-away stabilizer to wrong side of fabric. Or fuse interfacing to wrong side of the fabric.

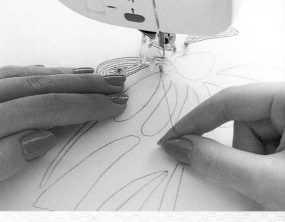

Bring bobbin thread to wrong side at beginning and end of stitching; knot top and bobbin threads together. Trim, leaving short tails if sewing single layer. If sewing through multiple layers, thread tails through tapestry needle and hide them between layers. Avoid backstitching or stitching in place.

Attach open-toe presser foot for sewing utility patterns, decorative patterns, straight-line stitching, or any machine-guided designs.

Attach darning presser foot for free-motion stitching. (Front of foot has been cut away for better visibility.) Lower or cover feed dogs, or adjust stitch length to 0, if feed dogs cannot be lowered or covered.

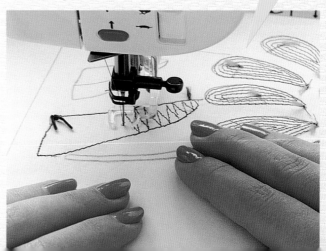

DOUBLE-NEEDLE STITCHING

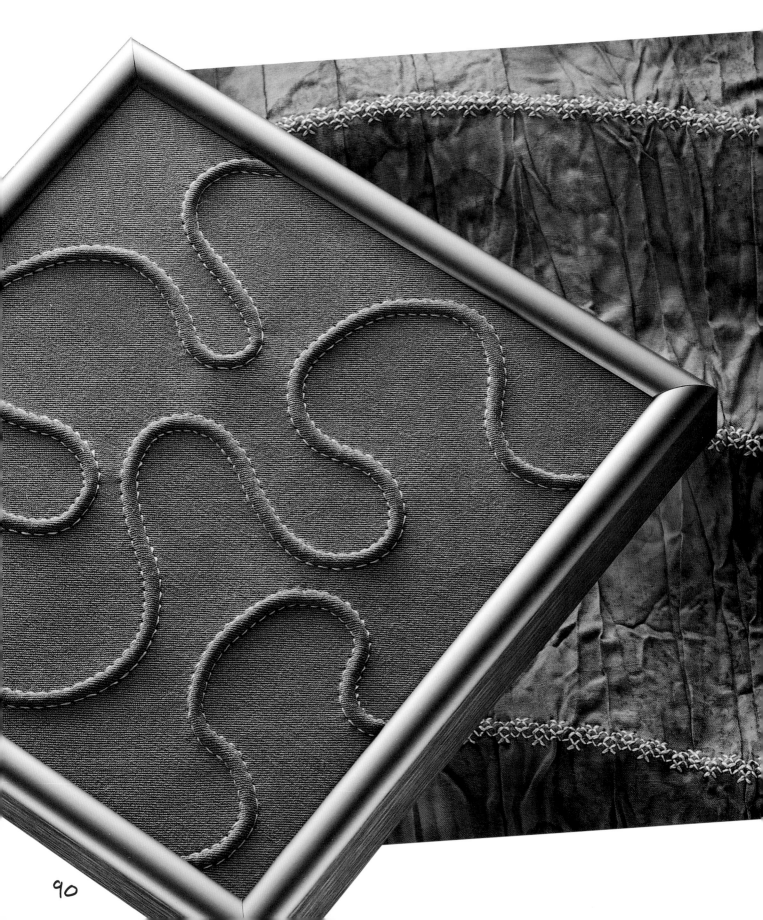

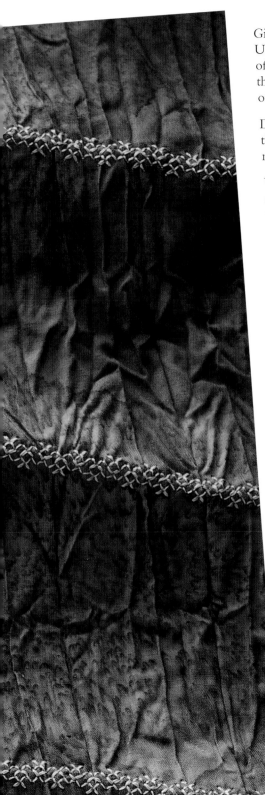

Give your fabric added dimension and design interest with double-needle stitching. Using decorative threads, stitch over texturized or pleated fabric with scattered rows of double-needle stitching. Stitch quilted effects, using a double needle to give the fabric a distinctive character. Create depth and texture with meandering trails of wide double-needle stitching, forming ridges over the fabric.

Double-needle labeling indicates the space between the needles, followed by the needle size. The range suitable for most machines includes needles from 1.6 mm/80 to 6.0 mm/100.

Widely separated double needles are suitable for straight stitching. Narrower double needles can be used with some decorative machine stitches, provided the width of the stitch allows the needles to clear the throat plate and presser foot openings. Always test the stitches carefully, turning the handwheel to avoid breaking the needles or damaging the machine.

TIPS FOR DOUBLE-NEEDLE STITCHING

Pull needle threads through to the wrong side at beginning and end of stitching lines; tie off securely with bobbin thread.

Use an embroidery foot for straight or decorative stitches that lie flat on the surface of the fabric; use a pintuck foot when stitching parallel rows of ridges.

Tighten bobbin tension slightly or use heavier thread in the bobbin, to create a more pronounced ridge on right side of the fabric. Tighten needle tension slightly if no ridge is desired.

Stabilize wrong side of lightweight or stretchy fabrics with fusible knit interfacing or freezer paper, for better stitch quality.

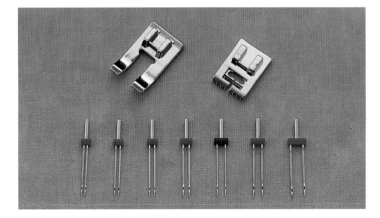

Cutout bottom of open-toe embroidery foot rides over ridges or decorative stitches. Pintuck feet have several cutout slots; select double needles to match slot widths.

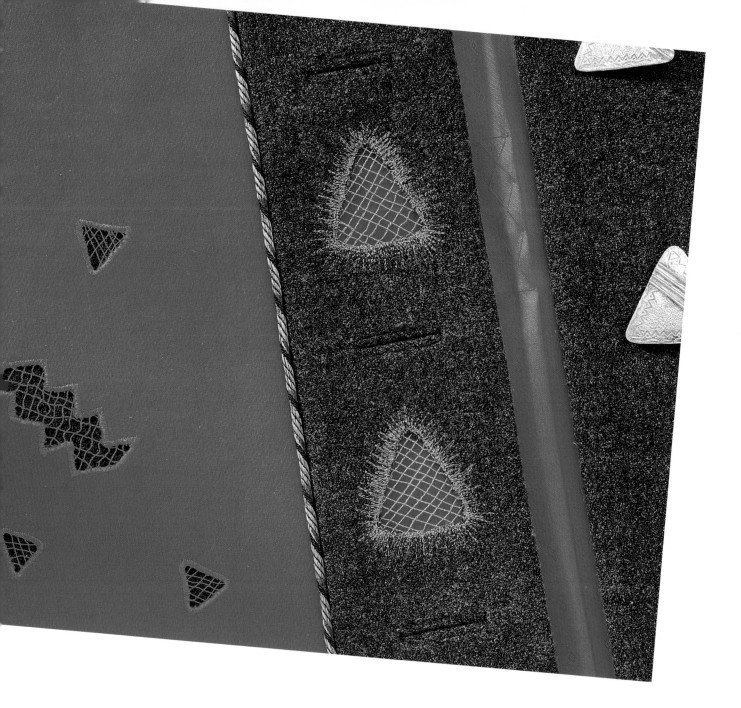

••• MACHINE OPENWORK •••

Create intriguing designs with machine openwork. Layered over contrasting fabric, openwork invites a peek into the "hidden" underlayer. Or openwork can be used alone to give a lacy effect to the fabric. For best results, select a closely woven fabric that does not ravel excessively, or stabilize ravelly fabric with lightweight knit interfacing. Cut out simple shapes, such as irregular circles, ovals, or freeforms. Set your machine for free-motion stitching as on page 181. Attach a darning foot, and thread the machine with the same thread in the needle and bobbin; decorative threads work well for this technique. Check your machine for balanced tension. Because you will be constantly rotating the hoop, it is easiest to work this technique on relatively small pieces of fabric.

Materials

- Fabric.
- Lightweight fusible knit interfacing, optional.
- Fine decorative threads, suitable for both needle and bobbin.
- Wooden embroidery hoop.
- Darning foot.

1 Fuse lightweight knit interfacing to wrong side of fabric, if fabric tends to ravel. On right side, draw outlines of openings, using removable marker or fine chalk line. Place fabric in hoop (page 182), stretching fabric taut.

2 Prepare machine as described opposite. Slide hooped fabric under darning foot. Stitch free-motion straight stitch three times around each marked outline, stitching over previous stitches with each pass.

3 Remove hooped fabric from machine. Cut out inside of one shape, using small sharp-pointed scissors. Cut as close as possible to stitches.

4 Slide hooped fabric back under darning foot. Stitch in place for a few stitches at top edge of stitched shape.

(continued)

HOW TO SEW MACHINE OPENWORK (continued)

5 Stitch across opening to opposite side, stitching at medium speed. Move hoop smoothly and steadily. Stitch just past outline stitches.

6 Stitch along outside edge of shape to another point; turn hoop so you will be stitching toward yourself.

STITCH PATTERN IDEAS

Stitch lines at erratic angles to each other.

Alternate stitching lines perpendicular to each other forming "plaid."

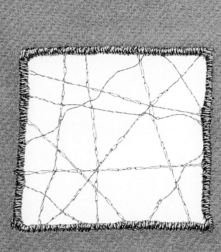

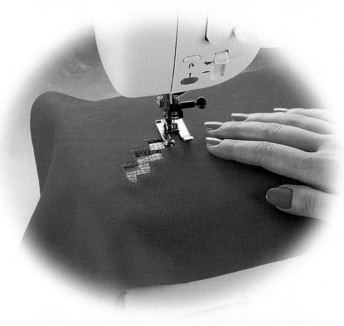

7 Repeat steps 5 and 6 until opening has been filled with desired amount of stitching lines, in desired pattern. Finish outer edge of shape with free-motion stitching or machine-guided decorative stitching in desired pattern.

8 Repeat steps 3 to 7 for each shape.

Intersect all lines at center like the spokes of a wheel.

THREAD LACE ▪ ▪ ▪ ▪ ▪ ▪

Lacy dimensional fabric can be created from decorative threads, using free-motion machine stitching techniques (page 181) and heat-sensitive stabilizer (page 218). Rather than stitching the design directly onto the garment fabric, a design is drawn onto the stabilizer. Free-motion stitching fills the design areas with decorative threads, in essence "painting a picture" with thread. The stitching may build a weblike filigree of thread for an airy, see-through appearance, or the stitches may fill areas quite solidly. A combination of stitching methods produces an intricate, dimensional finished design.

It is essential that all areas of the design connect to one another with stitching in order for the design to remain intact once the stabilizer is removed. After removing the stabilizer, the remaining thread lace can be applied to a garment or used for home decorating purposes in a number of innovative ways. Used alone, thread lace doilies or coasters are an elegant accent. Strips of thread lace can be used in place of fabric in pieced sections, or used as fringe along the edge of a garment, curtain, or fancy linens.

Materials

- ◆ Heat-sensitive stabilizer.
- ◆ Fine decorative threads, suitable for both needle and bobbin.
- ◆ Decorative machine sewing threads, such as rayon or cotton embroidery thread or metallic thread.
- ◆ Heavier threads, suitable for decorative bobbin stitching.
- ◆ Soft brush.

HOW TO ■■■■■■ SEW THREAD LACE

1 Trace or draw design onto heat-sensitive stabilizer. Wind desired heavy thread onto bobbin; set machine for decorative bobbin stitching (page 88). Working from wrong side, outline major design elements, using free-motion decorative bobbin stitching. Change thread colors as necessary.

2 Set machine for free-motion straight stitching. Working from right side, fill in design elements with small overlapping loops and circles. Change thread colors as necessary.

3 Fill in background areas around major design elements with small overlapping loops and circles, catching edges of design elements with stitches.

4 Add accent lines of free-motion straight stitches or loops and circles as desired. Add any design elements that will hang free, like fringe, along lower edge.

5 Remove stabilizer, following manufacturer's directions. Brush away residue with soft brush. Press lightly from wrong side.

97

Emboss rayon velvet with shimmery designs, using flat, heat-resistant objects. Create interesting textures by embossing the velvet with various wire meshes, such as wire fencing material or hardware cloth. For great results with motif embossing, use flat wooden cutouts, ⅛" to ¼" (3 to 6 mm) thick, available in any craft store in a wide assortment of shapes and sizes. Use embossed velvet in small doses for an accent on pieced garments. Emboss large areas of the velvet to create unique decorator fabric.

Materials

- Rayon velvet.
- Heat-resistant embossing material, such as wire, flat metal hardware, hardware cloth, rubber stamps, or flat wooden cutouts.
- Iron; press cloth.
- Flat, hard raised surface, such as a block of wood.
- Spray starch.

HOW TO EMBOSS RAYON VELVET ▪ ▪ ▪ ▪ ▪ ▪ ▪

1 Place embossing material on flat, hard surface. Place velvet facedown over embossing material.

EMBOSSED VELVET ▪ ▪ ▪ ▪ ▪ ▪ ▪ ▪

2 Apply liquid spray starch moderately and evenly over area of velvet to be embossed.

3 Cover velvet with press cloth, if desired. Apply steady, even pressure with hot, dry iron, pressing only in areas over embossing material. Reposition iron as necessary, lifting it straight up from surface; hold for 10 seconds in each area.

DEVORÉ ■ ■ ■

Fiber Etch® fabric remover, manufactured by Silkpaint Corporation, is used in innovative ways to create *devoré,* or cutwork effects, on plant fiber fabrics. The acidic nontoxic clear gel dissolves plant fibers, such as rayon, linen, cotton, and ramie. It does not affect protein fibers like wool or silk, or any synthetic fibers. This allows you to create interesting effects on some blended fabrics that contain 50% plant fiber and 50% synthetic or protein fiber, provided the method of blending involves weaving the fabric with one fiber in the warp and the other fiber in the weft.

Prewash the fabric to remove any sizing or other finish that will prevent the Fiber Etch from working or alter the results. Outline areas to be removed with satin stitching, using polyester or silk thread or metallic thread that has a synthetic base. Stabilize the fabric, using water-soluble stabilizer, paper, or starch. For best results, sew satin stitches at least 1/16" (1.5 mm) wide and tightly spaced with no fabric showing between the stitches. If you prefer, outline areas by using fabric paints or by attaching embellishments with adhesives. Because the gel dissolves the plant fiber, it is very important to read and follow the manufacturer's directions and test this technique on your fabric. Pressing is necessary to activate Fiber Etch, so if it is accidentally applied to the wrong area, sprinkle it with baking soda and wash it out with soap and water while it is still damp.

HOW TO USE FIBER ETCH FOR CUTWORK

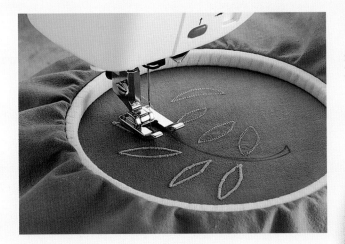

1 Mark design on fabric. Place fabric in hoop, if desired. Place stabilizer under fabric. Reinforce design with three close rows of short straight stitches. Satin stitch over straight stitches. Remove stabilizer.

2 Protect work surface with newspapers or paper towels. Apply thin layer of Fiber Etch gel to right side of fabric, in areas to be removed. Dry areas, using hair dryer.

3 Heat iron to setting suitable for fabric. Place fabric facedown on terry towel to avoid flattening satin stitches or other surface embellishment. Press treated areas, using dry iron, until areas become brittle.

4 Rinse under running water, rubbing gently to remove fibers. Allow to dry.

MORE IDEAS
FOR DEVORÉ

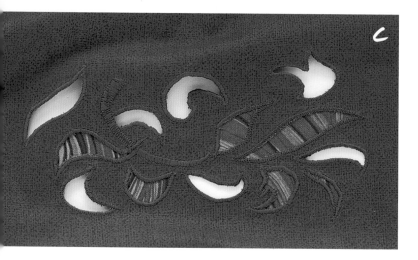

Computer-stitched cutwork (a). Avoid using Fiber Etch® in adjoining areas, since computer-stitched designs usually do not have reinforcing straight stitches around design elements.

Reverse appliqué (b). Place plant fiber fabric over synthetic or protein fiber fabric, right sides up. Satin stitch design, stitching through both layers. Apply Fiber Etch as in steps 1 to 3 on page 101. Fiber Etch removes only top layer, exposing bottom layer.

Reverse appliqué with cutwork (c). Sandwich two sheets of water-soluble stabilizer between two layers of plant fiber fabric, both faceup. Satin stitch desired design, as in step 1 on page 101, omitting further stabilizer. Apply Fiber Etch only to top layer to reveal second layer. Apply Fiber Etch to both top and back to produce cutwork.

No-sew techniques (d). Outline desired areas, using fabric paint, or attach heat-resistant embellishments around desired areas, using fabric adhesive. Follow steps 2 to 4 on page 101.

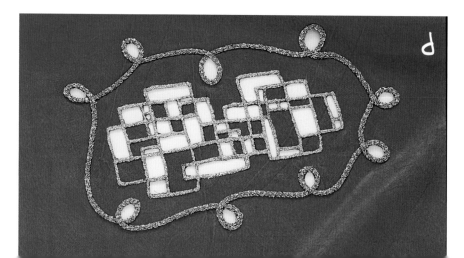

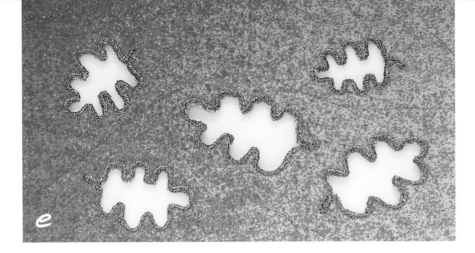

Quilted cutwork (e). Use 100% cotton batting between plant fiber fabrics. Satin stitch around desired areas. Follow steps 1 to 3 on page 101, applying Fiber Etch and pressing on both front and back sides. Fiber Etch removes both layers of fabric and the batting between them.

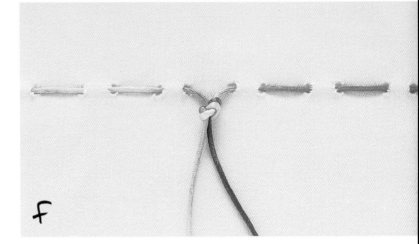

Frayed-edge cutwork (f). Apply Fiber Etch to small areas, without the confines of satin stitching, paint, or adhesives, for a casual, fraying edge.

Fabric blends (g). Fiber Etch removes only the plant fibers, creating an "etched" look.

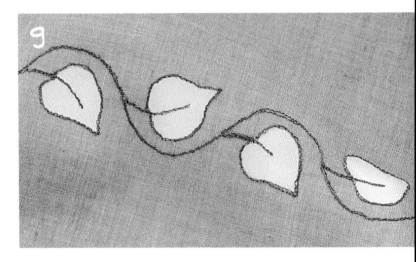

Etched velvet (h). This technique requires velvet with rayon pile and a silk backing. See source list on page 224. Apply Fiber Etch to the wrong side of the velvet, using a stencil or drawing with tip of applicator. Allow to dry, or dry with hair dryer. Place velvet over second piece of velvet, right sides together. Heat-activate with dry iron, using minimal pressure. Rinse fabric to remove pile.

Julann Windsperger

Part 2:
COLOR & DESIGN

Artists'
GALLERY #2

A creative spirit is caged
in every heart. The artist is the
one who eagerly unleashes
that spirit, lets it run wild, and
proudly parades it around town.
Be inspired!

AMY EVENSON MORRIS

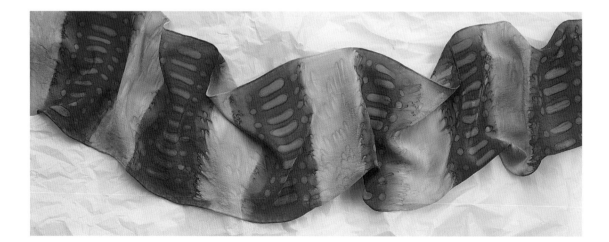

■ ■ ■ ■ ■ ■ ■ ■ ■ ■ ■

Amy Evenson Morris spends her days making fiber art and caring for her two children. Her fascination with silk painting and surface design began as a natural outgrowth of a love for other fiber arts, including knitting and quilting. She sells her original designs directly to clients from all over North America. Amy used a metallic gold resist in the serti technique to dye the square silk scarf at left. In the silk crepe de chine scarf, below, she used a combination of techniques with sea salt and alcohol to create the interesting patterns.

W endy Richardson has found a niche for herself overdyeing commercially printed fabrics in a low-water immersion process. She sells her visually rich fabrics, garments, patterns, and quiltworks at quilt shows and art fairs around the country and in Europe. Wendy herself is an accomplished quilter; she has won numerous awards and is represented at museums and in private collections.

WENDY RICHARDSON

ANNA CARLSON

A nna Carlson designs, creates, and embellishes coats, jackets, vests, and coordinates that combine beautiful colors and excellence in construction with an artist's sensitivity. She is fascinated by rich and varied surfaces; thus, her work involves the layering of color, piecing, appliqué, and stitching to create surfaces that invite a closer look and a touch. Her garments have simple classic lines that showcase the fabric, embellishments, and impeccable detailing.

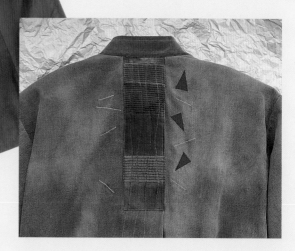

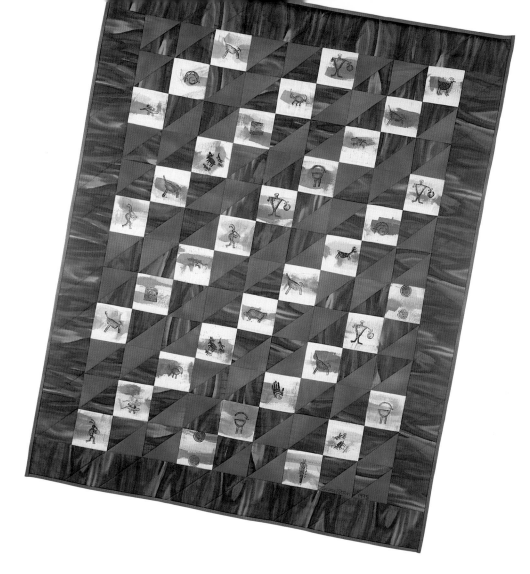

SUSAN STEIN

Susan Stein began to explore the world of quilting in 1977. What began as a hobby soon turned into a passion, as Susan charted a path that led her into many roles. She has owned quilt shops, taught classes, and served as state guild president. From her home, she sells quilts in two galleries while pursuing her interest in contemporary quilt design and writing a book on innovative Double Wedding Rings. Hand-dyed fabrics are integral to many of her quilt designs. She also incorporates stamping and other painting techniques that give her quilts their one-of-a-kind personality.

DIANE BARTELS

D iane Bartels has the ability to combine abstraction and reality with color and depth to create fabrics that are admired and cherished for their artistic merits alone. Along with a variety of dyeing methods, she uses a wide range of printing techniques in her textile art: screen printing, stamping, stenciling, and high-tech computer processes. This quilt exhibits some of her less complex, yet artistically fascinating, designs created by sun printing and hand-dyeing. Diane was a major contributor of research for this book. Her fabrics are also shown on pages 5, 134, 135, and 136.

REBECCA YAFFE

Rebecca Yaffe began her art career as a theatrical scene painter, working in several states across the country. She owns and operates Rebecca Yaffe Designs, where she designs, dyes, and paints fabrics for clothing and interiors. Her work, shown in galleries and exhibits locally and nationally, includes a line of fabrics created for a private label clothing collection. Shown above are a hand-dyed, hand-painted, and sprayed raw silk shirt and wall covering, and close-up views of Rebecca's hand-dyed, hand-painted jacquard silk scarves.

LAURIE SCHAFER

Laurie Schafer describes her signature technique for creating unique, sumptuous artwear as "stained glass appliqué." Working mainly with silk dupioni, she designs eye-popping appliqué designs on a framework of black fabric. While employing many couture techniques, Laurie adds a personal touch to many of her pieces by embellishing the lining with a song, poem, or message done in gold calligraphy.

PEGGOTTY CHRISTENSEN

Peggotty Christensen's vivid, original garments begin as white silk. With an inspired hand, she creates bold, colorful designs, using fiber-reactive dyes. Many of her designs are influenced by the beauty and tradition of the American Southwest, where she lives. Previously a metalsmith and jewelry designer for 30 years, Peggotty began her transition to textiles in the late 1980s, finding that both mediums shared many of the same design elements. She likens the layering of color on silk to the layering of different metals to create jewelry.

NANCY EHA

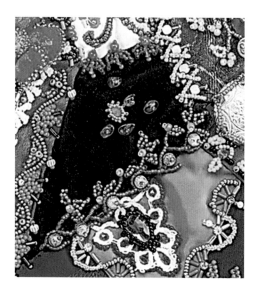

Nancy Eha is a nationally known beadwork artist, teacher, and author who encourages participants to go beyond the lure of color, sparkle, and beauty of beadwork, and reflect on the title or subject matter of her art. Many of her beadwork pieces require at least 50 hours of labor, with the goal of being juried into national exhibits. Nancy continually challenges herself to develop new beading techniques, include unusual objects, and provide an element of surprise in every piece.

N atalia Margulis is a native of Russia where, since childhood, she learned and developed skills in all kinds of hand and machine needlework. Her extensive travels and studies of Russian folk arts are the basis for her artistic interpretations of hand embroidery techniques into free-motion machine embroidery. Natalia "paints" thread on fabric, following her own patterns or designing as she stitches. Now an American citizen, her creations have won numerous awards and made her a sought-after teacher.

NATALIA MARGULIS

PENELOPE TRUDEAU

■ ■ ■ ■ ■ ■ ■ ■ ■ ■

Penelope Trudeau creates expressive wall hangings and garments, using various hand-dyeing and painting techniques, adding appliqués, embroidery, and beadwork.

The elaborate network of couched threads and beadwork on this quilt is carefully choreographed to accent and echo the dramatic color dance of the dyes, created by friend and fellow fabric artist, Gail LaLonde. Penelope found the process, though intricate and very time-consuming, to be a thrilling challenge and one of her most creatively satisfying projects.

The hand-dyed, screen-printed silk noile on page 122 is another example of Penelope's work. Penolope's work is also featured on page 22.

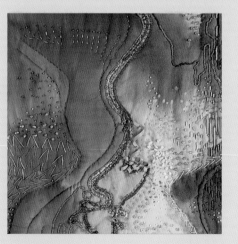

JULANN WINDSPERGER

Julann Windsperger finds time outside of her nursing career to create hand-dyed and painted fabrics which she turns into one-of-a-kind garments like this three-piece ensemble, which won first place at the Minnesota State Fair. It features several immersion-dyed fabrics that are also screen-printed and stamped. The outer vest, made of cotton velveteen, is machine-quilted for added texture. Julann's work is also featured on page 20.

SUSAN FRAME

Susan Frame utilizes some rather unique methods for painting and dyeing fabric, creating interesting effects using common materials. For instance, the garment shown here was first stamped using a rock from the shore of Lake Superior, dipped in thickened red dye. The surrounding areas were painted with thin dyes and a paintbrush. Susan, who began painting more than 25 years ago, specializes in Sumi-e (Asian brush painting) on rice paper and silk. She has adapted the techniques to silk fabric painting and developed her own couture fashion line.

JAYNE BUTLER

Jayne Butler has a passion for fabric sculpture and free-motion machine embroidery. She often incorporates decorative yarns and threads or interesting found objects to create dimension and texture. In the purse at right, she featured a heated and texturized recycled soda can. Throughout her life, sewing has always been a main focus, thanks in great part to her mother, who taught her to sew and encouraged her creativity. In her native Australia, Jayne studied under Dutch couture, Greta Amiet. She is a member of many sewing and machine embroidery organizations and the winner of numerous awards. Jayne shares her knowledge and enthusiasm for creative sewing through her nationwide workshops.

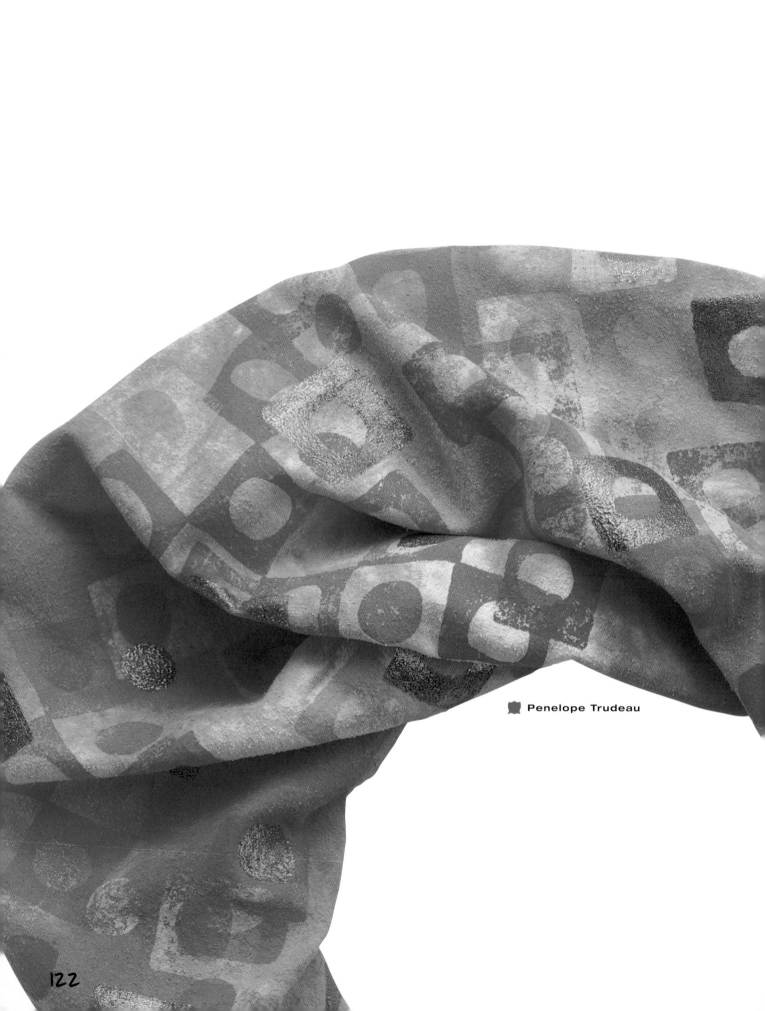

Penelope Trudeau

Dyeing & Design
TECHNIQUES

Have you ever dreamed of being a textile designer? Simple technology and innovative products to make that dream come true are now at your fingertips.
Start exploring!

FABRICS

Selection and preparation of the fabric you wish to color are two very important steps in the success of your project. There are several things to consider, depending on the techniques and products you intend to use. These include fiber content, weave structure, surface texture, and color.

Fiber-reactive dyes, for instance, are formulated to work well on cellulose fiber, such as cotton, linen, ramie, rayon, tencel, or jute. They also work well on silk, which is a protein fiber. The dyes do not work on synthetic fabrics, though it is possible, but not predictable, to get satisfactory results on fabric blends high in cellulose fibers. Cellulose fibers are also the choice for discharging dye, since bleach has no effect on synthetics, and it damages protein fibers, like wool and silk.

For painting on fabric, the surface texture and tightness of the weave, more than the fiber content, will affect the outcome. Surface texture inherent in the weave of the fabric will naturally affect applications such as stamping, stenciling, or photo transfer. The tighter the weave and smoother the surface, the less the image will be distorted.

You can purchase fabrics that have been prepared for dyeing at some quilt shops, specialty fabric stores, or through mail order sources (page 224). These fabrics are free of any impurities or finishes that would interfere with the dyeing or painting process. They may not, however, have been preshrunk. Avoid permanent-press, stain-repellent, or water-resistant finishes. These finishes, which will inhibit dyes from bonding or paints from adhering, are extremely difficult to remove. To prepare other fabric for dyeing or painting, wash it in hot water with Synthrapol® (page 129) and soda ash (page 129), using ¼ teaspoon (1 mL) of each per yard (0.95 m) of fabric. Do not use fabric softener in either the washer or dryer.

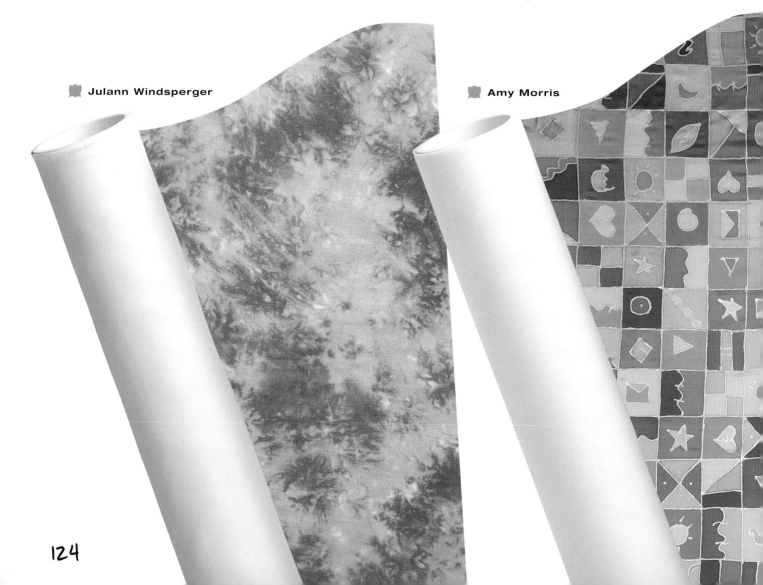

Julann Windsperger

Amy Morris

124

Lastly, consider the fabric's color. Dyes, some paints, and photo transfers are transparent, so the base color of the fabric will affect the coloring process. White fabric is essential if you want to dye fabric to match a color card. Even unbleached muslin adds a yellow element to the outcome. Dark and bright colors work best for discharging. White or pastels are recommended for photo transfers.

Occasionally some great finds are discovered in remnant piles, and the fabric may not be labeled. If you are unsure of the fiber content, ravel off a few yarns, roll them into a ball, and hold them with tweezers as you burn them. Compare the results to the descriptions, right. If you are a fabric stockpiler, as many of us are, be sure to label the fabrics you buy with information about specific fiber content, finishes, and whether or not it has been prepared for dyeing. You'll eliminate some guesswork, trial, and error later on.

Tests to Determine Fiber Content

Cotton, linen, and rayon fibers burn vigorously, with an afterglow. They burn with the odor of burning paper and leave a soft, gray ash.

Wool and silk fibers burn slowly and char, curling away from the flame. They sometimes burn only while in the flame. They burn with the odor of burning hair or feathers and leave a crushable ash.

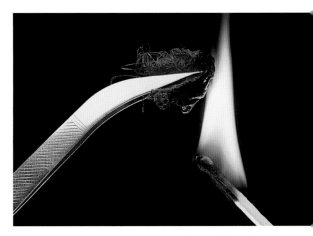

Polyester, nylon, and other synthetic fibers burn and melt only while in the flame, or shortly after being removed. They burn with a chemical odor and leave a hard bead.

PLAYING WITH COLOR ░░░░░░░░

Unless you are already an expert on color, your least threatening approach to the subject is to learn as you go. Enjoy the experimenting process, and rate your attempts on a scale of "oops!" to "smashing success," remembering that even the most undesirable results have taught you something. Seek the reactions of others as well, because the interpretation of color is very personal; one artist's "oops!" may be another's "smashing success."

Increase your odds of achieving success with an understanding of basic color theory. Refer to the color wheel for a visual guide when planning a color scheme for your fabric. The *primary colors*—red, yellow, and blue—are the three foundation colors of the wheel. All other colors are combinations of these colors, and they are the only three colors that cannot be achieved by mixing others. The *secondary colors*—green, orange, and violet—are the colors you get when you mix two primary colors. *Tertiary colors* result when you mix a primary and a secondary color. *Complementary colors* are located directly across the color wheel from each other.

It is important to keep in mind that the color wheel explains color in a very simplified form, based on the colors of light. Mixing dye or paint colors is a bit more complicated, because some colors are stronger than others in *value:* their lightness or darkness. For instance, you will not get a true secondary green by mixing equal parts blue and yellow. Blue paint or dye has a darker value and is much more influential in the relationship, so the green color you want is best achieved by mixing blue into yellow, a small amount at a time.

Intensity refers to the strength or purity of the color. The pure colors form the outer ring of the color wheel. The intensity of a color is lessened by adding a small amount of its complementary color, thus creating a *tone*. *Shades* are achieved by mixing black into a color; blue plus black equals navy blue. *Tints* are achieved by mixing white into a color; red plus white equals pink. This makes sense for paint, but there is no such thing as white dye. White fabric showing through transparent dye creates the tint. The amount of dye powder in the dye bath determines the degree of the tint.

The most interesting color schemes include elements with various values. *Monochromatic color schemes* are made up of tints, shades, and tones of the same color, usually a sure success. *Analogous schemes* include colors that are adjacent to each other on the color wheel, and may include various tints, shades, or tones of each. A good rule of thumb when designing a fabric with a *complementary color scheme* is to use one of the colors predominantly and its complement as an accent color. Also, keep in mind that dyes and some paints are transparent. If you stamp a yellow transparent paint design over a violet background, the design will turn a muddy brown. An opaque yellow paint or flowing lines of yellow embroidery, however, will result in the complementary scheme you intended.

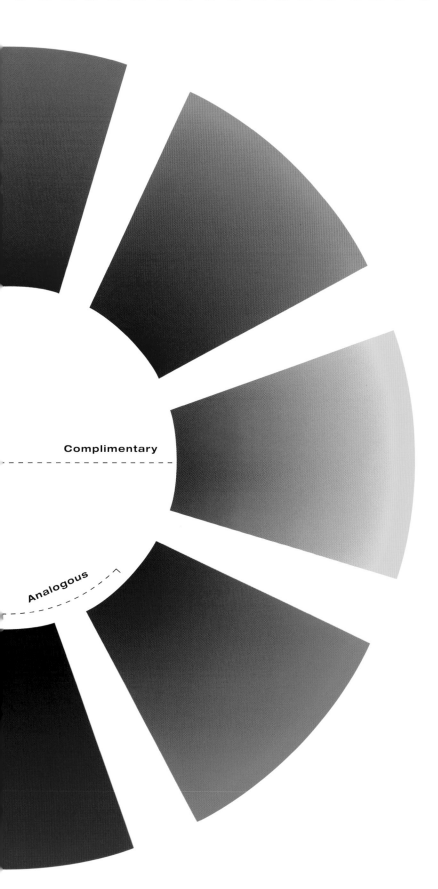

Complimentary

Analogous

Monochromatic

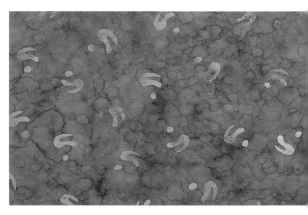

Complementary

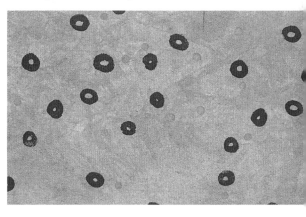

Analogous

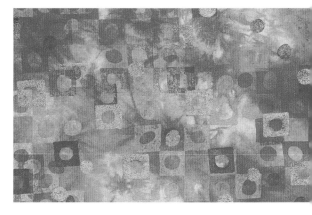

DYES

Fabric dyes give you the capability of achieving rich brilliant color, subtle shading and highlighting, and watercolor blended effects without changing the hand of the fabric. Browse through mail-order catalogs and you will find a wide assortment of dyes in powder or liquid form, some developed for specific techniques and others versatile enough to be used for almost anything. There are even dyes available in crayon and marker forms, putting instant color capability at your fingertips. Read the manufacturer's directions and experiment with different forms and brands to discover your own favorites.

One of the most popular dyes is Procion® MX, a fiber-reactive powdered dye, mixed and used at room temperature. It is formulated for dyeing natural-fiber fabrics: cotton, rayon, silk, or wool. The term "fiber-reactive" means that during the dyeing process, a chemical reaction occurs, permanently bonding the dye molecules with the fiber molecules. In essence, the dye becomes part of the fabric. This results in brilliant color that cannot wash out or rub off.

Along with the dye powders and water, there are a few other products necessary to mix and use fiber-reactive dyes. *Synthrapol,* used to prewash fabric to remove any sizing, dirt, or other impurities that would inhibit dyeing, is also used in the final wash to remove any loose dye particles. *Soda ash fixer,* commonly known as sodium carbonate, is a mild alkali that facilitates the chemical reaction between the dye and the fibers. *Urea* is an organic nitrogen that keeps the fabric wetter longer, allowing the chemical reaction to take place. *Calsolene oil* is a liquid wetting agent that increases the saturation power of the water and consequently the dye. A thickener, called PRO Print Paste Mix SH, available from PRO Chemical and Dye, Inc. (page 224) can be added to the dye to make it suitable for direct applications, like stamping or screen printing.

Dyeing methods include *immersion,* used when you want to dye a piece of fabric all one color, and *low-water immersion,* which results in a one-color or multicolor textured look with variations in value. Low-water immersion can also be used to overdye printed fabrics. Fabric dyed with either of these methods provides a wonderful canvas for further color and design work, including *direct dye application,* where multiple dye colors can be applied in a variety of methods and consistencies. In immersion dyeing, the soda ash is added to the dye bath, activating the chemical reaction. For direct application methods, the fabric is presoaked in the soda ash water, and either hung to dry or spread out damp or wet for applying the dye. The chemical reaction begins when the dye touches the fabric in the presence of the soda ash.

For most applications, the dye powder is first mixed with water in a concentrated form. The recipes and directions that follow are only general guidelines. Dye manufacturers provide information for determining the amount of dye powder required to dye specific amounts of fabric to match each color in their color cards. Keep a detailed notebook of the recipes and dyelots used in each dyeing session, if you want to be able to repeat hues, values, and intensities.

Though the Procion dyes are nontoxic, certain precautions should be taken when using them. Always wear a dust mask when mixing the dye to avoid inhaling the powder. Wear rubber gloves and use utensils and containers for mixing and storing dyes that will not be used for food. Keep all mixtures well-labeled and away from children and pets. Unused dye mixtures or exhausted dye baths can safely be poured down the drain without harming the environment.

Materials

- Natural-fiber fabric, prepared for dyeing (page 124); up to 3 yd. (2.75 m).
- Washing machine; dryer.
- Large plastic bucket; wooden or plastic mixing spoons.
- Rubber gloves; dust mask.
- 1½ gallons (5.75 L) water.
- 1½ cups (375 mL) noniodized salt.

- Procion® MX fiber-reactive dye powder (2 to 8 teaspoons per 1 lb. [10 to 40 mL per 500 g] of dry fabric, according to manufacturer's recommendations).
- Soda ash; water.
- 1 teaspoon (5 mL) Calsolene oil.
- Synthrapol.

1 Prepare fabric for dyeing (page 124). Dissolve salt in lukewarm water in large bucket; add Calsolene oil. Dissolve dye completely in 1 cup (250 mL) of warm water; add to bucket, and stir to distribute evenly. In separate container, prepare soda bath (below); set aside.

2 Put thoroughly wet fabric into dye bath. Stir fabric almost constantly for 20 minutes. Pour 2 cups (500 mL) soda bath, small amounts at a time, into dye bath, stirring constantly; avoid pouring directly onto fabric. Allow fabric to remain in dye bath ½ hour to 1 hour, depending on color intensity desired; stir occasionally.

3 Remove fabric, pour dye bath down drain; it is not reusable. Set machine for warm wash/warm rinse; put fabric in filled machine, and allow to run through cycle. Reset machine for hot wash/warm rinse, add Synthrapol (¼ teaspoon [1 mL] per yard [0.95 m] of fabric), and wash. Machine dry.

Soda Bath

1 cup (250 mL) soda ash
1 gallon (3.8 L) hot water

Mix until completely dissolved; allow to cool to room temperature.

Dye Concentrate

2½ tablespoons (37.5 mL) urea
½ cup (125 mL) warm water
1 tablespoon (15 mL) dye powder

Mix well. Label and store in refrigerator when not in use.

Dye Concentrate to Water Ratios

Dark: 6 tablespoons to 10 tablespoons (90 to 150 mL)

Medium: 3 tablespoons to 13 tablespoons (45 to 195 mL)

Light: 1 tablespoon to 15 tablespoons (15 to 225 mL)

Pour dye concentrate in measuring cup; add water to make 1 cup (250 mL).

Materials

- Natural-fiber fabric, prepared for dyeing (page 124); up to 3 yd. (2.75 m).
- Washing machine; dryer.
- Large plastic bucket.
- Large plastic vat or dishpan; wooden or plastic mixing spoons.
- Rubber gloves; dust mask.
- 1½ gallons (5.75 L) water.

- 1½ cups (375 mL) noniodized salt.
- Procion MX fiber-reactive dye powder (2 to 8 teaspoons per 1 lb. [10 to 40 mL per 500 g] of dry fabric, according to manufacturer's recommendations).
- ⅙ cup (42 mL) soda ash.
- 1 teaspoon (5 mL) Calsolene oil.

1 Prepare fabric for dyeing (page 124); tear into manageable pieces, ½ yd. to 1½ yd. (0.5 to 1.4 m). Dissolve salt in lukewarm water in large bucket; immerse fabric. In separate container, prepare soda bath (opposite). Prepare dye concentrates (opposite).

2 Remove fabric from salt water; wring out excess. Arrange single layer of fabric in bottom of vat; scrunch as necessary to fit. Dilute dye concentrate with water following ratio guide, opposite. Pour over fabric, distributing evenly; use 1 to 2 cups (250 to 500 mL), depending on amount and thickness of fabric. Allow to sit for 10 to 15 minutes.

3 Pour soda bath over fabric, using about half as much soda bath as you used of dye mixture; distribute evenly. Allow to sit for 1½ hours. Remove fabric from vat; pour dye mixture down drain. Rinse and wash fabric as in step 3, opposite.

Materials

- Natural-fiber fabric, prepared for dyeing (page 124).
- Plastic drop cloth; large plastic plates.
- Procion MX fiber-reactive dyes, in desired colors.
- Urea.
- Soda ash.
- Synthropol.
- String, rubber bands, or clothespins, for "tying" fabrics.
- Measuring spoons, cups, plastic spoons, for mixing dyes.
- Rubber gloves; face mask.
- Zip-lock plastic bags.

1 Mix thickened dye (above) as necessary for technique. Prepare fabric for dyeing (page 124). Immerse fabric in soda bath (page 130); allow to soak for 20 minutes. Remove fabric; wring out excess water. Hang to dry or use wet or damp as technique requires.

Thickened Dye

5½ tablespoons (82.5 mL) PRO Print Mix SH

1 cup (250 mL) water

Add print mix slowly to water, stirring constantly. Thin, if desired, adding urea water (7 teaspoons. [35 mL] urea to 1 cup [250 mL] water) in small amounts. Allow to sit overnight. Mix equal parts with dye concentrate, for dark value. Adjust ratio for lighter values. Mix only as much as you will use in one session.

2 Cover work surface with plastic drop cloth. Spread fabric on surface; secure with tape or T-pins. Apply dye to fabric using paintbrush, foam applicator, roller, or other technique, such as stamping (page 136), stenciling (page 142), or screen printing (page 146). Cover fabric with sheet of plastic. Roll up layers, and allow fabric to cure at room temperature for at least 24 hours.

3 Unroll fabric; remove plastic. Rinse in cool water, then warm water, gradually changing to hot water, until water runs clear. Machine wash, using Synthropol; machine dry.

Silk dyes. Stretch silk on wooden frame. Apply liquid silk dyes in desired colors and pattern; allow to dry. Apply rubbing alcohol in desired areas to create highlights; use paintbrush, foam applicator, or cotton swab, or drip alcohol on silk. Allow reaction to take place; dry. Steam-set (page 163).

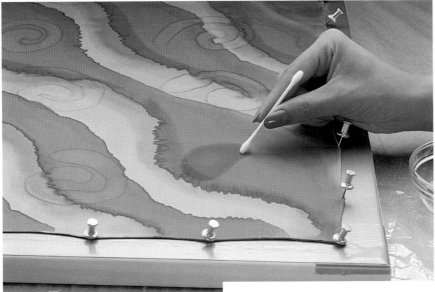

Dye sticks and markers. Draw directly on fabric, using dye sticks or markers. Overlap colors to blend. Shade a color, using its complementary color (page 126). Allow to dry. Heat-set, following manufacturer's directions.

FABRIC PAINTS

Painting is one of the easiest methods of putting color and design on fabric. Fabric paints are basically pigments attached to binders or adhesives. When you paint on fabric, the binders adhere the pigments to the fibers. Fabric paints may change the hand of the fabric in varying degrees, depending on the brand, type, and consistency of the paint you use.

Fabric paints are available in both opaque and transparent types. Transparent paints allow the fabric's print or color to show through, and are suitable anytime you want a sheer, color-washed look. Opaques cover the surface completely, making them ideal for painting on dark or black fabric. Pearlized or metallic paints dry with a lustrous appearance.

Paints can be used in their natural consistency or diluted with water. There are various consistencies available, each suited to particular application techniques. For instance, paints suitable for screen printing have the consistency of pudding; those used for painting on silk are like water.

METHODS FOR PAINTING ON FABRIC

Diane Bartels

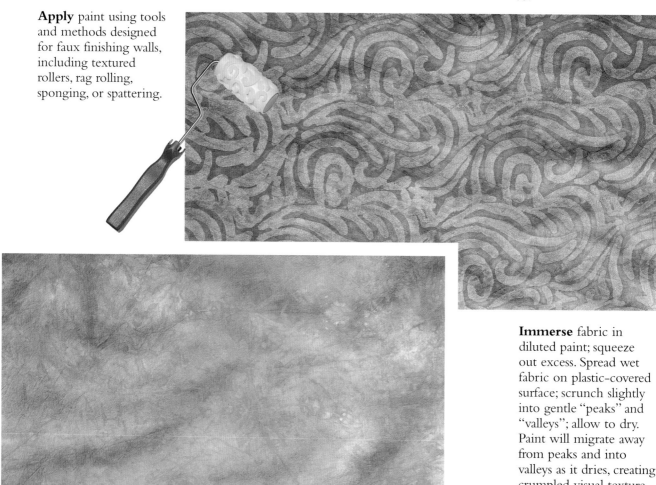

Apply paint using tools and methods designed for faux finishing walls, including textured rollers, rag rolling, sponging, or spattering.

Immerse fabric in diluted paint; squeeze out excess. Spread wet fabric on plastic-covered surface; scrunch slightly into gentle "peaks" and "valleys"; allow to dry. Paint will migrate away from peaks and into valleys as it dries, creating crumpled visual texture.

Aside from the specific techniques of stamping (page 136), stenciling (page 142), and screen printing (page 146), paints can be applied to fabric in countless ways. Experiment with paintbrushes, rollers, foam applicators, sponges, feathers, fingers, syringes, sprayers, or any method imaginable. For ease in application, tape fabric to a slightly padded surface, protected with a plastic drop cloth.

Natural-fiber fabrics are recommended for painting techniques, though some synthetic blends are suitable also, as long as they can withstand the high heat necessary to set the paint. Prewashing the fabric in hot water and mild detergent removes any sizing that may have been applied during manufacturing, optimizing the paint's ability to adhere to the fibers. Twenty-four hours after air-drying, heat-set the painted fabric, pressing with a dry iron from the wrong side or using a press cloth. Though fabric paints can be dry-cleaned and are fade-resistant, they may rub off with repeated washing or friction, so wash gently to preserve the color and design.

Diane Bartels

Apply ribbons of diluted paint in harmonious colors to wet fabric, using foam applicator or squirt bottle, for watercolored effect. Sprinkle kosher salt in wet paint to create interesting texture. Salt draws in pigment, creating tiny darker spots surrounded by pale halos. Allow to dry completely before moving.

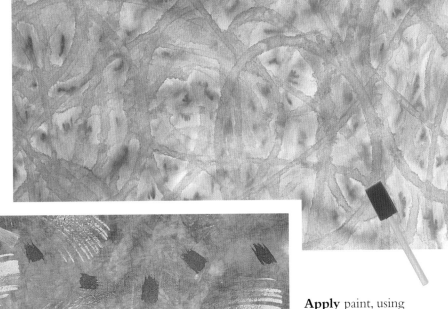

Apply paint, using various artist's brushes. Use stiff-bristled brushes to apply thicker paints. Thin paint slightly with water to apply with softer brushes.

STAMPING

With a little imagination, many household items become tools for stamping designs on fabric. Try a wooden spaghetti lifter, flat metal hardware items, plastic bubble wrap, or a ball of string. Small objects, such as buttons, coins, or keys, can be glued to the end of a wooden dowel, empty film container, or large cork for easy stamping. In fact, cork itself can be cut into interesting shapes for printing fabric. Some items are more easily used for stamping if they are not mounted to a surface. Cellulose sponges cut into shapes produce wonderful textured effects. Leaves, flower petals, or grasses may be used to produce whispy, nature prints. And don't forget your vegetables!

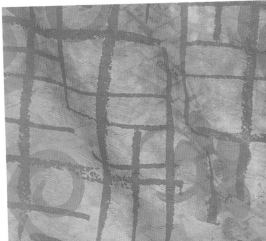

Purchased stamps, particularly those with less fine detail work, are also useful for stamping on fabric. Printing blocks can be cut from a number of materials, including white artist's erasers or larger blocks made of the same material, available at art supply stores. These blocks are easily cut with a mat knife or linoleum block cutters. Any closed cell foam material, including neoprene sheets, insulation tapes, or computer mouse pads can be cut into shapes with scissors and attached to a block for printing. Art supply stores also carry adhesive-backed sheets of closed cell foam, designed for this purpose.

The weave structure of the fabric plays a large part in the clarity of the printing. Obviously, the clearest results are obtained on tightly woven fabric with fine yarns. The looser the weave and the larger the yarns, the more distorted the stamped image will be.

Use any fabric paints, inks, or dyes to stamp the images on fabric. Also, use this stamping technique for applying resists (page 151) or for discharging dye (page 169) to create a stamped image. Follow the manufacturers' directions for using the products and for setting the stamped images permanently in the fabric.

Secure small items such as coins, buttons, or metal washers to dowel ends, bottle corks, or empty film containers, using silicone glue.

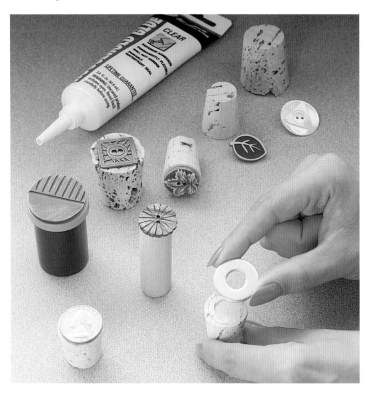

Spread wood glue on wood block. Arrange uniform layer of rope, cording, or string in desired design in wet glue; allow to dry. Or secure ribbed fabric, corrugated cardboard, or other textural material. Print design on paper; adhere to top of block, to aid in positioning stamp.

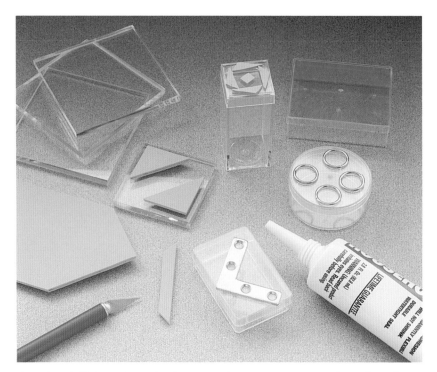

Cut clear ¼" (6 mm) acrylic sheet into shapes or use empty clear plastic boxes in assorted sizes for see-through printing blocks. Cut layered self-adhesive foam into desired shapes; mount to blocks. Mount other items using silicone glue.

HOW TO MAKE A PRINTING BLOCK ■■■■■■■■■■■■
FROM ARTIST'S ERASER MATERIAL

1 Draw design on surface of block material or transfer design to surface using transfer paper. Cut about ¼" (6 mm) deep into block along outer design lines, using mat knife.

2 Remove large background area around design by cutting horizontally through edge of block up to cuts made for design outline.

3 Cut and remove negative areas within design, cutting at an angle along each edge.

Linoleum cutter method. Carve away negative areas of design, using linoleum cutting tools. Follow manufacturer's directions for using tools. Some styles are pushed to cut; others are pulled.

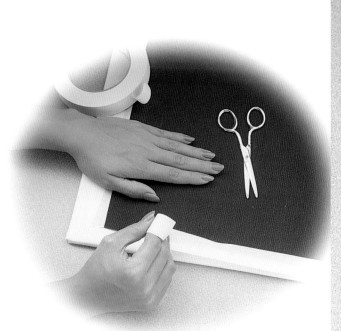

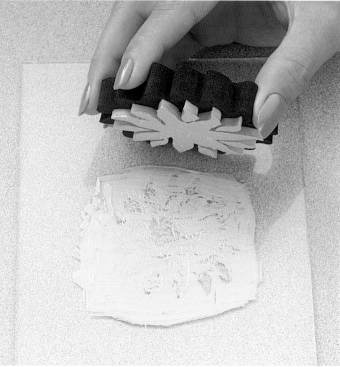

Place fabric to be stamped over smooth, padded surface, such as muslin layered over foam-core board. Stretch taut, and secure with masking tape around edges.

Apply thin layer of fabric paint to smooth surface, such as sheet of glass. Press stamping material onto surface to pick up paint for stamping. Recoat surface as needed.

Apply paint or ink directly onto stamping surface, using foam applicator. This allows you to print multicolored designs.

Make a stamp pad by placing several layers of felt on a smooth, flat surface; thoroughly wet, but do not saturate, felt with fabric dye, ink, or thinned paint (four parts paint to one part extender). Press printing block evenly into felt pad, lightly coating surface. Stamp fabric.

Reapply dye, ink, or paint after each stamp for designs of relatively same intensity.

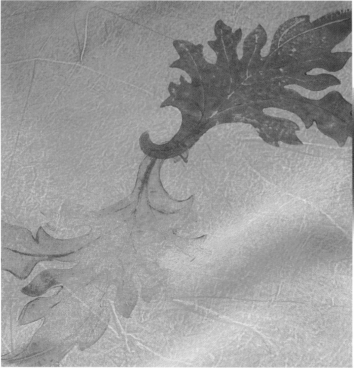

Brush paint onto uncut surface of artist's eraser or printing block. Remove paint to create a negative design, using a wipe out tool, pencil eraser, or corner of another artist's eraser. Print design onto fabric.

Stamp two or three times before reapplying paint or ink for designs with varying intensities, depth, and shading.

STENCILING ▪▪▪▪

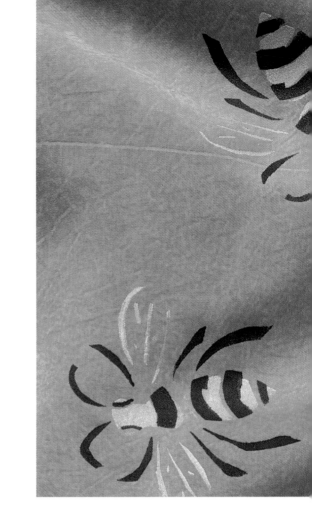

Stenciling produces single or repeated designs with gradations of color. A multitude of commercial stencils is available. Most commercial stencils have separate stencil plates for each color, numbered according to sequence of use. For stenciling fabric, avoid stencils with minute details that will be distorted or lost by the fabric grain. You may choose to design and make your own stencils or copy a design from another source, altering the size as needed.

Stenciling is a very versatile technique, suitable for a wide range of mediums, including fabric paints, dye sticks, resists, and bleach. With proper care and storage, stencils will last a long time.

Materials

- Colored pencils; paper.
- Transparent Mylar® sheets.
- Fine-point permanent marker.
- Mat knife; cutting surface, such as self-healing cutting board.

▪▪▪▪▪▪ HOW TO MAKE A CUSTOM STENCIL ▪▪▪▪▪▪▪▪

1 Draw or trace design; color in areas of design to be cut out, using colored pencils. If multiple plates are desired, color areas for each plate a different color. Mark placement guides.

2 Position Mylar sheet over traced design, allowing at least 1" (2.5 cm) border at top and bottom; secure with tape. Trace areas to be stenciled in first color, using marking pen. Transfer placement guides.

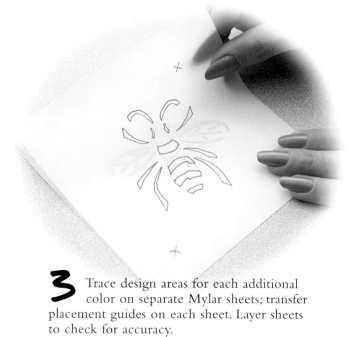

3 Trace design areas for each additional color on separate Mylar sheets; transfer placement guides on each sheet. Layer sheets to check for accuracy.

4 Cut out marked designs on each sheet, using mat knife. Pull knife toward you as you cut, turning sheet, rather than knife, to change direction.

Use stencil brush or foam applicator in size appropriate for stencil openings. Apply medium with dabbing or pouncing motion. Brushing motion may cause medium to leak under edges of opening.

Mask off openings as necessary, if more than one color will be applied using the same stencil plate.

Overlap stenciled images to create depth. Allow first layer to dry before stenciling second layer.

Vary the stenciled effect by using other tools to apply paint, such as sea sponge, cellulose sponge, or spray applicator.

Apply repositionable spray adhesive to back of stencil to help it stick to fabric.

Clean stencils thoroughly immediately after each use. Lay stencil flat; dab with wet sponge. Do not rub or brush. Allow to dry. Repair minor tears in the stencil with cellophane tape.

SCREEN PRINTING

Screen printing is another method for printing single or repeating images. Unlike the gradated and shaded images produced by stenciling, and the characteristic inconsistent images produced by stamping, screen-printed images feature crisp lines and total, even coverage. In this method, the design is prepared on a fine mesh screen using water-soluble Speedball® Screen Drawing Fluid and Screen Filler. The coloring medium is forced through the mesh with a squeegee, printing the fabric in the open areas of the design.

Art supply stores and mail order companies carry convenient ready-made printing screens in a variety of sizes. The screen consists of a wooden frame with finely woven fabric (silk or polyester) stretched tautly across one side. The mesh is sized according to the openness of the weave; the smaller the number, the more open the weave. Purchase multifilament polyester screens with 12xx mesh.

Water-based textile inks, created for screen printing, are used most often, though thickened dye and most fabric paints can be used also. For best results, the medium must have the consistency of pudding. Avoid paints that contain glitter, as the glitter will clog the screen. Besides printing images onto fabric, the screen printing method can also be used for discharging dye (page 169) from fabric or for applying a resist (page 151).

For best results, work on a smooth padded surface. Secure foam rubber and batting, several layers of muslin, or terry cloth to a large board and stretch muslin or an old sheet over it, making certain there are no wrinkles in the layers.

Materials

- Printing screen with 12xx multifilament polyester mesh in desired size.
- Duct tape.
- Speedball Water-soluble Screen Drawing Fluid and Screen Filler.
- Textile inks, textile paints, or thickened dye.
- Squeegee, ½" (1.3 cm) narrower than inside measurement of screen frame.
- Plastic drop cloth; padded work surface; paper towels.
- Fabric, prewashed and pressed.

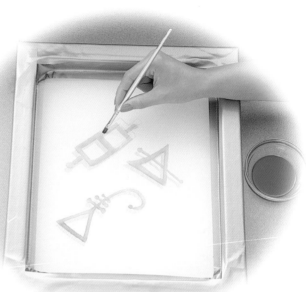

1 Wrap duct tape over all edges of wooden frame to waterproof it. Extend duct tape about ½" (1.3 cm) onto mesh on upper side of screen, forming a border or trough.

2 Elevate screen slightly off work surface. Position design pattern on surface under screen, if desired. Apply screen drawing fluid to mesh in areas you wish to print, using paintbrush or sponge applicator. Allow to dry completely.

3 Apply thin even coat of screen filler over entire screen, using squeegee as on page 148, steps 1 and 2. Allow to dry.

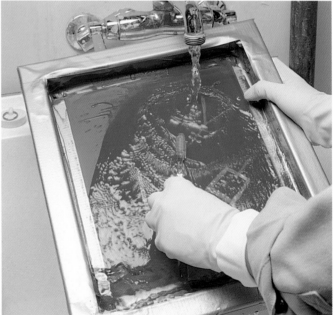

4 Spray cold water on both sides of screen, concentrating on areas where drawing fluid was applied. Screen filler will wash away in these areas; scrub lightly with small stiff brush, if necessary. Allow screen to dry thoroughly.

1 Secure plastic drop cloth tautly over padded work surface. Tautly secure fabric, right side up, over surface. Place screen over fabric. Place 2 to 3 tablespoons (30 to 45 mL) of print medium next to design area or along border.

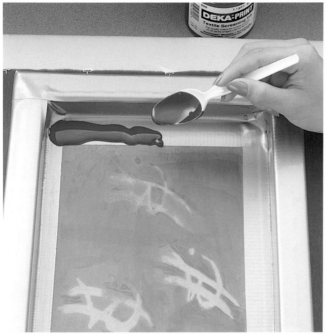

2 Press screen firmly against fabric with one hand. Applying firm, even pressure, pull squeegee across the screen, drawing medium across open areas of design. Hold squeegee at an angle, leaning in the direction you are pulling it. Scoop up excess paint with squeegee; deposit at top of screen. Repeat motion until medium is evenly distributed.

3 Lift screen slowly from fabric at an angle. Reposition screen and repeat process in another area, if desired. Avoid placing screen over wet medium. Work quickly so that medium does not dry on screen.

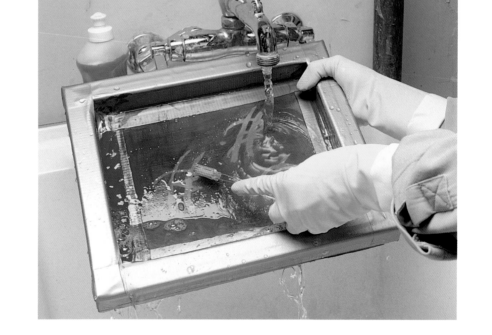

4 Wash screen with soap under warm running water immediately after printing. Dry screen completely before using again. Touch up blocked area with screen filler as necessary.

Allow screen-printed images to dry completely before printing over them a second time or before printing right next to them, so that frame of screen does not smudge adjacent images.

Apply two or more colors of ink or paint next to each other along the top of the screen to print an image with a blended color effect.

Screen print images over dry fabric that has been discharged (page 169), dyed, or painted with another technique, to create depth.

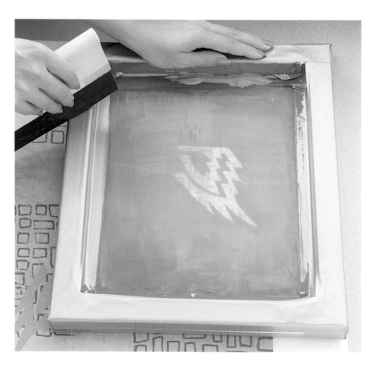

Prepare a separate screen for each design and color you wish to print to minimize the total printing time required. Print all of one color or design, and wash screen before proceeding to next screen.

149

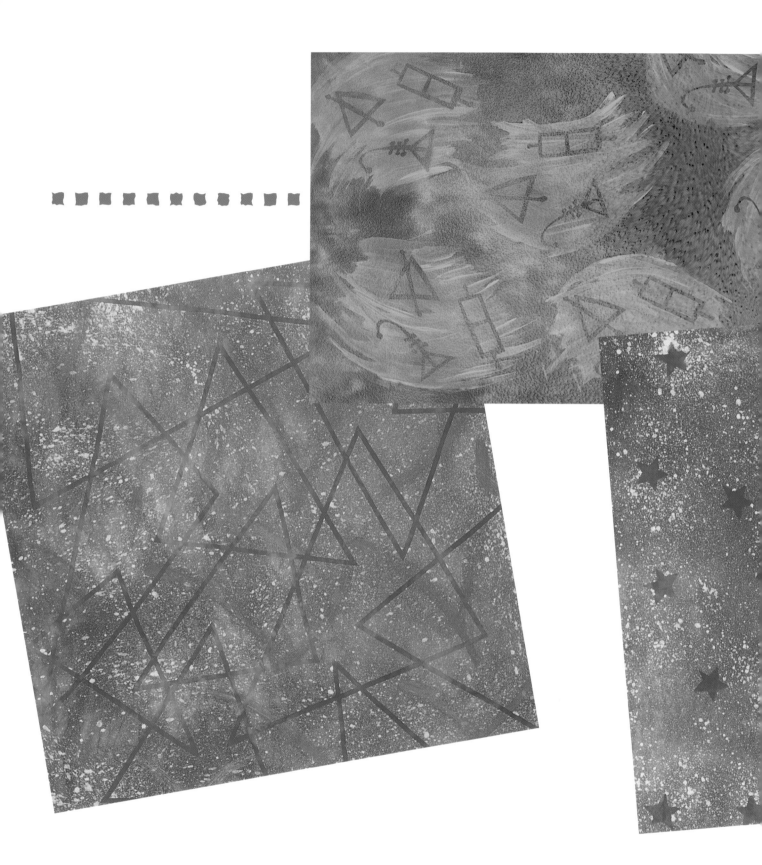

RESISTS

Just as the name implies, a resist is a means of creating a design by enabling the fabric to resist a dye, paint, or discharge solution. The design results from the negative colored space. Some resists are mechanical, meaning something is placed over the fabric or the fabric is manipulated in a way to prevent color medium from reaching certain areas. Leaves, paper doilies, or a plastic comb placed on the surface of the fabric to block sprayed paint, dye, or bleach are simple mechanical resists. Another common mechanical resist method is to fold, twist, or otherwise manipulate the fabric, securing it with rubber bands, clamps, or strings, thus prohibiting the color medium from reaching certain parts of the fabric.

Water-based resists are substances that temporarily coat the fibers, prohibiting them from accepting the color medium. These liquid resists are applied to the fabric by any means also suitable for fabric paint, thickened dyes, or bleach gel. They must be thoroughly dry to be effective, preferably for twenty-four hours. Because they are water-soluble, they are not suitable for coloring methods that wet the fabric, such as immersion dyeing. After painting or dyeing, the resist washes out, leaving a negative design (positive, when discharging). Water-based resists are available from art supply stores and catalogs. Follow the manufacturers' directions for specific use of their products.

The examples (right) were prepared using fabric paints. Similar effects can be created by direct application of dyes (page 132) over resists.

Mechanical Resists

1 Arrange items, such as leaves, buttons, wooden shapes, doilies, decorator trim, or anything that will provide interesting shape over surface of fabric. Dilute fabric paint to milky consistency; pour into household spray bottle. Spray paint over fabric in thin coats, allowing fabric to dry between coats. Angle of spray may create shadow effect behind resist object. Remove items; heat-set.

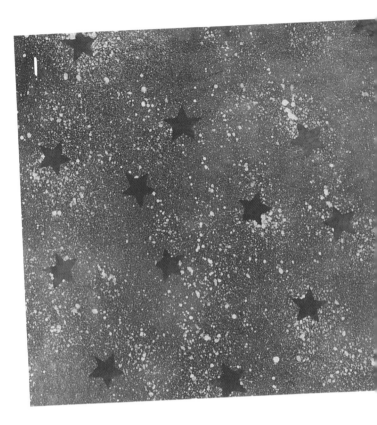

2 Fold, crumple, twist, stitch, or tie off fabric with rubber bands as for tie-dyeing (page 154). Apply diluted fabric paint; allow to dry. Smooth out fabric, and heat-set. Or prepare resist and apply bleach solution, using tie-dye methods; follow page 170, steps 1 to 3, to discharge dye in unique pattern.

3 Apply masking tape to fabric surface in desired design. Or cut a design from self-adhesive vinyl, and apply to fabric. Brush or spray fabric paint over surface of fabric. Allow to dry completely before removing resist; heat-set. This method creates sharply defined lines.

Water-based Resists

4 Apply water-based resist to rubber stamp or other item used for stamping; stamp fabric. Reapply resist after ever stamp. Allow resist to dry thoroughly. Apply fabric paint over stamped designs, using desired method. Allow to dry. Heat-set paint. Wash fabric to remove resist.

5 Apply water-based resist to fabric, using paintbrush, for broad strokes and large, filled-in areas. Use fine-tipped dispenser for applying narrow lines or handwriting. Allow to dry thoroughly. Paint fabric as desired; heat-set. Wash fabric to remove resist.

6 Apply resist, using screen-printing method, page 146. Allow to dry thoroughly. Apply fabric paint over screen-printed designs, using desired method. Allow to dry. Heat-set paint. Wash fabric to remove resist.

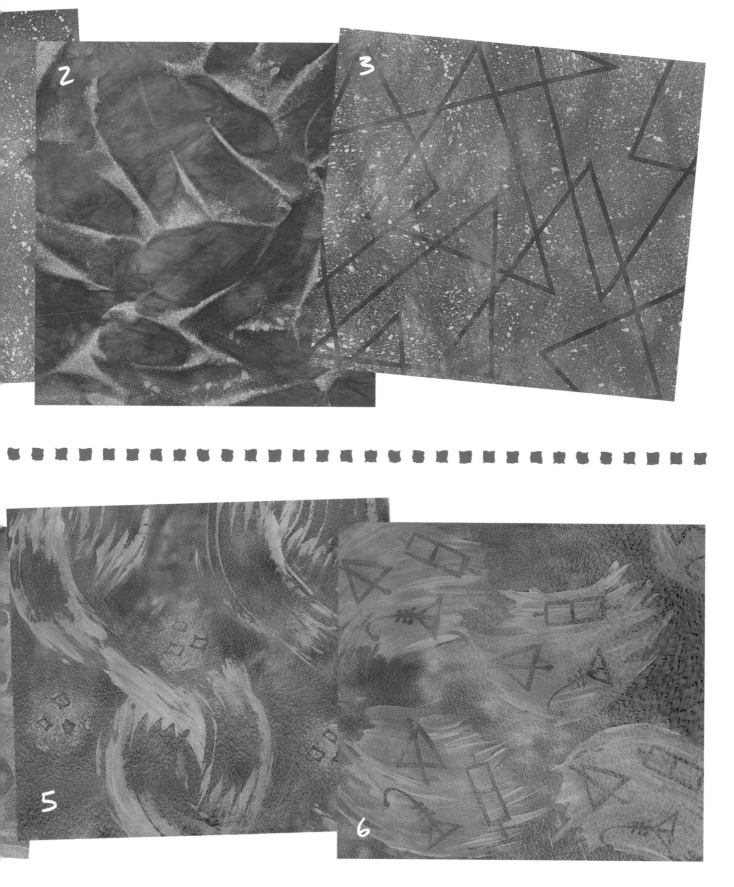

153

TIE-DYEING ● ● ● ● ● ● ● ● ● ● ● ● ● ● ● ● ● ●

All the rage in the '60s and still going strong, tie-dyeing is an everpopular method of obtaining vivid colorful designs on fabric. It's not just for T-shirts anymore, either. Quilters and garment artisans alike take advantage of the color explosions, patterning, and visual depth of tie-dyed fabric.

In simplest terms, tie-dyeing involves the manipulation of fabric by folding, twisting, scrunching, or stitching to create a resist (page 151) in certain areas, blocking them from receiving dye. Rubber bands, string, or clothespins are used to hold the manipulated fabric in place. In the direct application method taught here, dye is applied to the fabric by dipping, squirting, sponging, or brushing, depending on the desired effect.

The best tie-dyed results are achieved using 100% cotton or silk fabric that has been prepared for dyeing (page 124). Other natural fiber fabrics, like rayon and linen, can also be used. Work with manageable pieces, ½ yd. to 1 yd. (0.5 to 0.95 m) square, depending on the manner in which you intend to manipulate the fabric.

Review the information on color (page 126) to help you create combinations that work well together. Be aware that if you apply two complementary colors of dye right next to each other, the fabric may turn brown where the dyes overlap. Some secondary and tertiary colors of dye will produce a halo effect when their component colors penetrate the fabric at different rates. For instance, the blue component of a purple dye may separate out and spread farther into the fabric than the red component, creating a wonderful gradation from red to purple to blue. Experiment with different manipulations and dye combinations, and record your results, but don't be surprised if you have difficulty duplicating favorites.

Materials

- 100% cotton or silk fabric, prepared for dyeing (page 124).
- Plastic drop cloth; large plastic plates.
- Procion MX fiber-reactive dyes, in desired colors.
- Urea.
- Soda ash.
- Salt (canning or pickling).
- Synthropol.
- String, rubber bands, or clothespins for "tying" fabrics.
- Measuring spoons, cups, plastic spoons, for mixing dyes.
- Rubber gloves; face mask.
- Zip-lock plastic bags.

Soda Bath

1 cup (250 mL) soda ash

½ cup (125 mL) noniodized salt

1 gallon (3.8 L) hot water

Dye Solution

Mix:

½ cup (125 mL) hot water

1 tablespoon (15 mL) urea

Add and mix well:

1 to 8 teaspoons (5 to 40 mL) dye powder

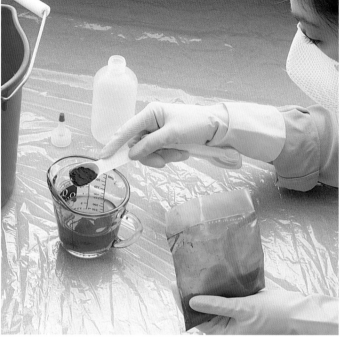

2 Mix dyes while fabric is soaking. Wear face mask to avoid breathing dye powder; wear rubber gloves.

1 Cover work surface with plastic drop cloth. Manipulate fabric as desired; tie or clamp, using rubber bands, string, or clothespins (pages 158 and 159). Prepare soda bath; soak fabric until saturated, about 20 minutes. Gently squeeze excess solution from fabric, but do not rinse.

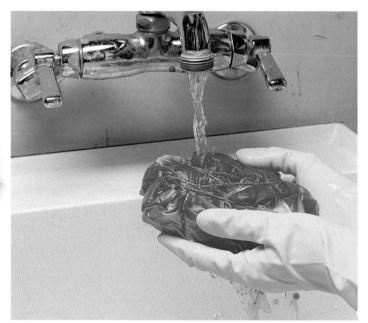

3 Place fabric on large plastic plate. Apply dye to fabric, using desired method (opposite); apply enough dye to penetrate fabric but not puddle on plate. Place tied, dyed fabric into plastic bag; close securely. Allow fabric to cure at room temperature 24 hours.

4 Remove fabric; rinse under running water until water is nearly clear. Untie fabric and rinse again. Wash by hand or machine, using ¼ teaspoon (1 mL) Synthropol per yard (0.95 m) of fabric; final rinse water should be clear. Hang to dry or machine dry. Fabric is colorfast and ready to use.

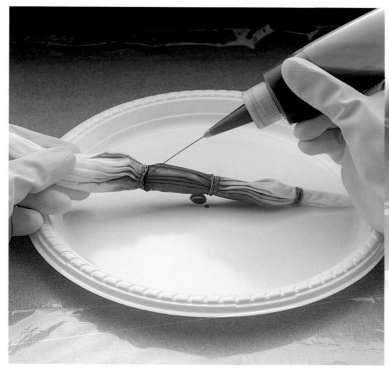

Dipping. Pour dye into shallow, wide bowl. Dip desired area of tied fabric into dye; allow excess dye to drip back into bowl.

Squirt bottle. Pour dye into squirt bottle, using funnel. Squirt dye on fabric in desired areas. Work tip of bottle into folds and crevices.

Foam applicator. Dip foam applicator into dye; brush onto fabric.

Rolled plaid. Fanfold fabric. Roll folded strip into fairly tight circle; tie. Apply dye to one flat side of circle; turn over and apply dye to other side. Use two different colors, if desired.

Stripes. Fanfold fabric. Crease folds if sharp lines are desired. Tie tightly with string or rubber bands at even or uneven intervals. Apply dye to fabric between ties. To dye a plaid pattern, complete page 156, steps 1 to 4, in stripe pattern. Then repeat, folding in opposite direction.

Fanfolded plaid. Fanfold fabric in one direction. Fanfold folded strip in opposite direction. Tie folded stack. Apply dye to folds around outer edges of stack.

Squares and triangles. Fanfold fabric in one direction. Fanfold folded strip in diagonal folds, forming triangular stack; tie. Apply dye to folds around outer edge of stack.

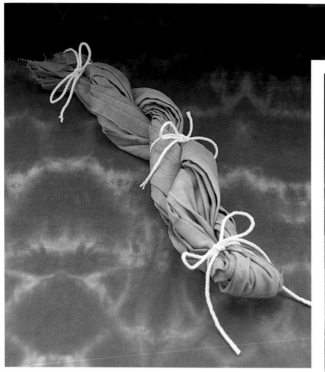

Scrunch. Lay fabric out flat on surface. Beginning at center, scrunch fabric into a shapeless, lumpy wad; tie securely. Apply dye randomly over all exposed surfaces.

Spiral twist. Loosely scrunch fabric length from one side to the other. Twist ends in opposite directions until fabric doubles over at center; tie. Apply dye randomly over all exposed surfaces.

Starburst. Fold fabric in half; mark center of fold. Beginning at fold, fanfold both layers together in triangular wedges radiating from center of fold; tie in several places from point to ends. Apply dye, alternating colors on folds and flat surfaces.

Gathering stitches. Stitch rows of basting stitches in desired pattern through fabric; use sturdy thread. Pull threads to gather; tie. Apply dye to exposed surfaces.

159

SERTI ▪ ▫ ▪ ▫ ▪ ▫ ▪ ▫ ▪ ▫ ▪ ▫ ▪ ▫ ▪ ▫ ▪ ▫ ▪ ▫ ▪ ▫

Serti is a resist technique that allows you to create dyed designs with distinct, hard lines. Most often used on lightweight China silk, but applicable to other fabrics, serti prevents the blending of the dyes from one area to the next by completely enclosing each design area with a thin line of resist. When applied to the silk, the dye spreads up to the resist, filling in the enclosed space, but going no farther. Brilliant color is best heat-set into the fabric, using a steaming method. After setting the dyed design, the resist is removed, leaving thin white or colored lines between distinct design areas.

Water-based resist, such as Silkpaint!® Resist, is tintable with dyes and easily removed with cool water. It is applied as a liquid, using a fine-tipped applicator squeeze bottle or a convenient tool, called The Airpen®, by Silkpaint Corporation.

The design you create or select should have distinct areas that can be completely enclosed by the resist. It may have additional accent lines that can also be covered with resist.

Materials

- Lightweight China silk, prepared for dyeing (page 124).
- Stretcher bar frame and silk tacks or push pins, or large wooden embroidery hoop.
- Wooden blocks for raising frame.
- Water-soluble resist.
- The Airpen, or fine-tipped applicator squeeze bottle.
- Silk dyes.
- Soft brushes or foam applicators, for applying dye.
- Unprinted newsprint; rubber bands.
- Deep kettle, steaming net or rack, terry towel, aluminum foil, for steaming fabric.

Amy Morris

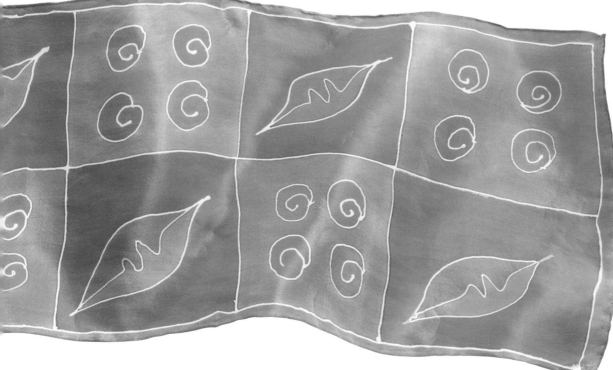

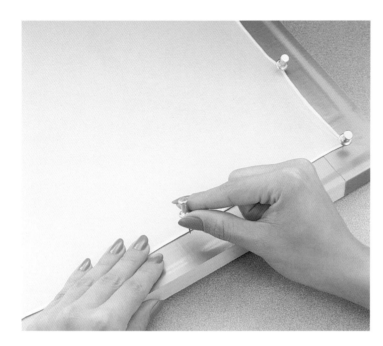

2 Place pattern on table, under silk. Add dye to resist, if color is desired. Pour resist into Airpen or applicator bottle. Apply resist to all design lines, following tips on page 164. Begin in one upper corner and work toward bottom of design to avoid smudging lines.

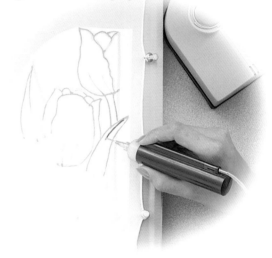

1 Wrap frame with duct tape to protect wood from dyes. Tack silk fabric to frame at corners, using silk tacks or push pins. Stretch fabric taut; secure on all sides, staggering placement of tacks, so none are directly across from each other. If silk dyes require any preparation, follow manufacturer's directions.

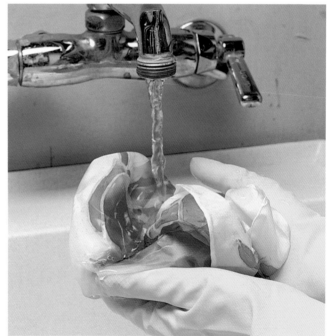

3 Apply dye, using brush or foam applicator. Follow tips for applying dye to silk on page 165. Use separate brush or foam applicator for each dye color. Allow fabric to dry completely.

4 Remove fabric from frame. Heat-set dyes using steam method (opposite). Rinse fabric in cool water to remove resist; allow to dry. Press.

1 Sandwich dyed, dry fabric between two or three layers of unprinted newsprint. Roll paper and fabric together into a loose bundle; secure bundle with rubber band. Newsprint keeps the dyes from migrating to other parts of the fabric.

2 Pour 2 to 3 cups (500 to 750 mL) of water in a deep kettle. Place bundle on steaming net or raised rack, several inches above water. Shape a dome of aluminum foil; place over bundle.

3 Place a folded terry towel over kettle to absorb excess moisture; place lid on kettle. Heat water to boiling; steam bundle for 30 minutes, turning bundle over after 15 minutes. Steam must rise and penetrate fabric, without getting fabric wet.

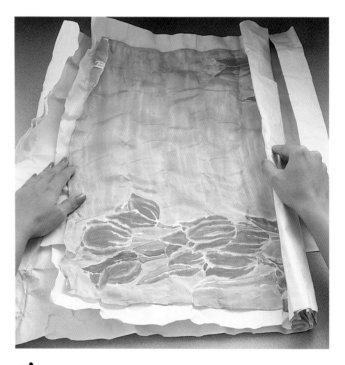

4 Remove from heat. Unwrap bundle immediately.

Applicator bottle method. Purchase metal-tip gutta applicator bottle for best results; it may be included with purchase of resist. Some have interchangeable tips for different line widths. Hold bottle vertically; press tip firmly against suspended fabric. Squeeze bottle and move along design lines at an even pace. Practice before applying resist to project.

Airpen method. Read manufacturer's directions. Assemble tool using tip in size suitable for desired line width. Cover air hole with index finger to release resist from pen; move tip steadily along design lines. Practice until you feel comfortable with tool.

Remove mistakes immediately with cool water. Press folded fabric to underside in mistake area; swab away resist from right side, using cotton-tipped swab.

Hold fabric up to light and check from underside to see that resist has penetrated fabric completely and that there are no gaps in resist lines. Every design section must be completely enclosed.

Raise stretcher bars or hoop higher off surface as wet fabric sags to prevent it from touching work surface. Or, remove silk tacks or push pins one at a time, and restretch fabric.

Dip tip of paintbrush or foam applicator in dye; touch to center of desired area. Allow dye to transfer from brush to fabric and spread toward resist. Ease dye toward outer edges of area as necessary; using tip of brush. Do not use a typical stroking motion. Use separate brush or applicator for each color.

Highlighting. Apply water to wet dye in an area you wish to highlight, using small clean paintbrush. Or, drag wet brush through area. Rinse brush and repeat as necessary.

Blending. Apply two different colors in one area, and allow dyes to run together. Wet area with water before blending for more subtle blending. Apply dyes to dry fabric for more controlled effect.

SUN PRINTING •••

Harness a little solar power to create stunning shadow designs on fabric. Special sunlight-reactive Setacolor transparent paints by Pebeo are so easy to use, even children will find this process fun and exciting. You simply brush the diluted paint onto the fabric, position the object that will resist (there's that word again) the sun, place the fabric in the sunlight, and wait. If you can't wait for a sunny day, you can use a halogen lamp or a sun lamp that emits ultraviolet light.

Begin with fabric that is all white **(1)**, already dyed **(2)**, or commercially printed **(3).** Almost any fabric will work, including cotton, polyester, cotton/polyester blend, silk, and linen. The finer the weave, the more distinct the shadow will appear. Dilute the Setacolor paint with water; two parts water to one part paint or up to eight parts water to one part paint. The more diluted the paint, the more transparent the color will be, and the more faint the shadow will appear.

Materials

- ◆ Finely woven fabric, as described above.
- ◆ Hard, flat surface, such as plywood, foam core, or heavy cardboard.
- ◆ Setacolor paints; bowl for diluting paint; foam applicator.
- ◆ Objects for resisting the sun, such as leaves, feathers, wooden shapes, metal or plastic washers, lace, paper cutouts, anything with an interesting shape.
- ◆ Sunlight, or other suitable light source.

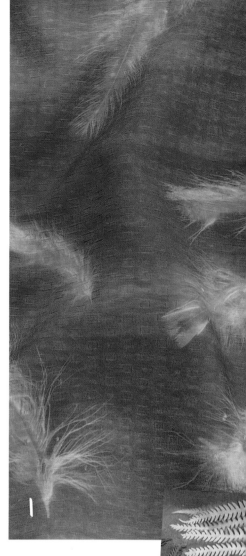

HOW TO MAKE A SUN PRINT

1 Stretch fabric taut over a smooth, waterproof, transportable surface; secure outer edges with tape or pins. Dilute desired colors of Setacolor transparent paint. Spread paint on fabric, using foam applicator; cover fabric entirely.

2 Place opaque objects (resists) on wet fabric. For best results, objects should lay flat on fabric. Move fabric to sunny, still spot. Allow fabric to dry completely.

3 Remove resists. Heat-set fabric by pressing it, facedown, at temperature appropriate for fabric. Or preheat oven to 210°F (99°C), then turn off oven. Place fabric on aluminum foil in oven for 10 minutes. Wash, dry, and press fabric.

DISCHARGING DYE

Discharging is a fast and relatively easy method for creating designs by removing dye from colored or printed fabric. Bleach applied to the fabric begins to remove color immediately and continues to do so until the fabric is rinsed in cold water and neutralized. For best results, the bleach should be allowed to work no longer than ten minutes. After rinsing, the fabric must be immersed in a vinegar/water bath to neutralize the bleach. Because the bleach works fast, prepare the cold water bath before you apply the bleach. The rinsing and neutralizing can be done in buckets for small pieces of fabric, or in the washing machine for larger pieces.

Designs are created in the fabric by discharging the dye from certain areas while leaving the remainder of the fabric its original color. This can be done in several ways, depending on the desired results. For some methods, household bleach is simply diluted with water in a 50/50 solution and applied to the fabric with a foam brush, sprayed over the fabric surface, or squirted out of a syringe. For more control, use a thickened bleach, readily available in the form of household cleaning gels or dishwashing gel, such as Sunlight®, Comet®, or Clorox Cleanup®. To speed up results, add up to 50% more bleach to these gels. Apply the gel to the fabric, using a printing block (page 136), stencil (page 142), or screen (page 146). A mechanical resist (page 151) can be incorporated by pleating, folding, or twisting the fabric in any of the methods on page 158 before applying the bleach.

Select dark or brightly colored rayon or cotton fabrics for the most profound results. Bleach damages protein fibers like silk and wool. Prewash, dry, and press the fabric before discharging the dye. Work in a well-ventilated area, and wear rubber gloves and protective goggles. If you are spraying the bleach solution, the ideal conditions are to work outdoors with a breeze at your back. Cover the work surface with plastic and wear old clothes because you will inevitably get a stray drop of bleach where you don't want it.

Because the results are unpredictable and permanent, test each fabric before proceeding to determine what color or colors your fabric will become and how long to leave the bleach on the fabric to get the desired results. You may be surprised at the colors that are produced with the discharging process. Dark blue fabric, for instance, may turn various shades of pink or peach. If you enjoy the challenge of creating without guarantees or controlled results, discharging may be the method for you.

2 Watch discharging process carefully. When desired effect has been reached, gently transfer fabric into cold water bucket; rinse thoroughly. Or, transfer fabric into washing machine and turn on to run through wash cycle. Clean any tools, stencils, or screens thoroughly to remove all traces of bleach.

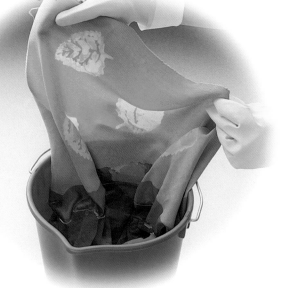

1 Cover padded work surface with plastic. Prepare bucket of cold water for rinsing. Prepare bucket of neutralizing solution, mixing 1 cup (250 mL) white vinegar in 1 gallon (3.8 L) water. Or, fill washing machine with cold water. Apply bleach solution or gel to fabric using one of the methods opposite.

3 Squeeze out excess water. Transfer fabric to neutralizing solution; allow to soak for ½ hour, agitating occasionally. Or, pour 1 cup (250 mL) white vinegar into washing machine as it begins rinse cycle. Squeeze or spin out excess solution. Hang or machine dry fabric.

Stenciling. Apply bleach solution or gel over stencil, using foam applicator, sponge, or synthetic stencil brush. Bleach solution works well for textured fabrics or pile fabrics, such as cotton velveteen. Bleach gel is recommended for smooth, tightly woven fabrics.

Stamping. Apply thin, even coat of bleach gel to stamp or other item, using foam applicator. Reapply gel after each print.

Work on 1 yard (0.95 m) or less of fabric to obtain multiple images with relatively equal results. Work in random pattern, rather than progressing from one end of fabric to the other; designs applied first will have more profound results than those applied last.

Place desired items over fabric surface to create mechanical resist (page 151). Spray fabric with bleach solution, using household spray bottle. Wear protective clothing, goggles, and mask.

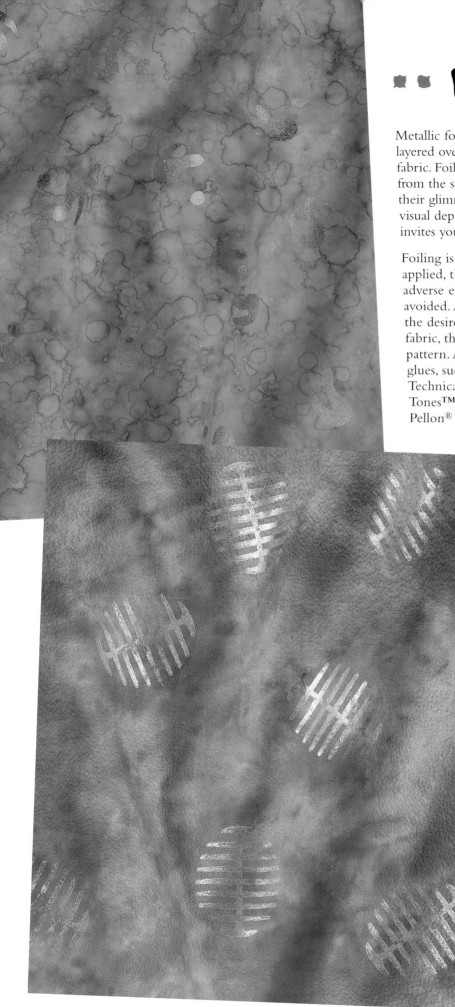

•• FOILING ••

Metallic foil designs offer a crowning touch when layered over the top of artistically dyed or painted fabric. Foil has a smooth glimmering quality, different from the subtle glint of metallic paint. Aside from their glimmering richness, foiled designs also add a visual depth and contrast that catches your eye and invites you to look closer.

Foiling is a relatively easy technique and, once applied, the foiled fabric can be laundered with no adverse effects. However, dry cleaning should be avoided. An adhesive is first applied to the fabric in the desired area. When ironed facedown onto the fabric, the metallic foil adheres to the adhesive pattern. Adhesives include washable, flexible fabric glues, such as Stitchless® and Jewel Glue™ by Delta Technical Coatings and Plexi® Glue by Jones Tones™. In another method, fusible web, such as Pellon® Wonder-Under™, cut into shapes, is used to bond the foil to the fabric. Suitable foils must be intended for use on fabric. See the source list on page 224.

Glue can be applied to the fabric in different ways, depending on the desired result. For the clearest, most consistent design, apply the glue by screen printing (page 146). Other suitable methods include stamping (page 136), brushing it on with a foam applicator, applying it through a squeeze bottle, or pouncing with a damp sea sponge.

Materials

◆ Adhesive in the form of glue (suitable brands listed above), or fusible web.

◆ Tools as desired, for applying glue.

◆ Foil intended for use on fabric.

◆ Iron; press cloth.

1 **Glue method.** Apply glue to fabric, using desired tools and techniques. Wash tools immediately. Allow glue to dry.

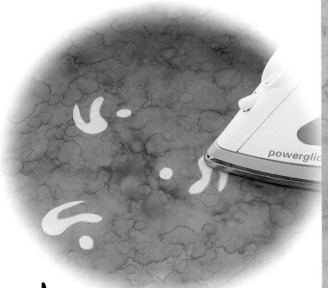

1 **Fusible web method.** Trace desired shapes on paper backing of fusible web; cut out. Fuse shapes to fabric, following manufacturer's directions. Remove paper backing.

2 Place foil, colored side up, over fabric; cover with press cloth. Press with iron set at high heat for 10 seconds in each spot. Allow to cool. Peel cellophane from foil. Repeat as necessary to foil all areas.

PHOTO TRANSFER ▪▪▪▪▪▪▪▪▪

If you have access to an inkjet printer or color copier, either at home or at the local copy shop, you can transfer photographic images to fabric for artistic applications. Actually, any image you can copy, scan, or create on your computer screen can be transferred to fabric with this method. With computer technology, scissors, and a creative mind, the application possibilities are endless. The memory craze is translated by quilters into heirloom quilts that depict photographic family history. Cloth dolls may carry photographic faces of real people. A cherished photo can be heat-set into the fabric cover of an album or diary. Memorable mountain views might adorn a favorite hiking jacket.

Basically, the photographic image is copied onto special transfer paper and then heat-set onto the fabric. This is done in one of two methods, using either a color laser copier or a color inkjet printer. You can access a color laser copier at most copy shops, where the image is simply copied onto the transfer paper. Check with the copy shop to see if you must furnish your own transfer paper and the specific kind of paper their copier requires. To use an inkjet printer, the photograph is first scanned into the computer and then printed out on transfer paper. Transfer papers are specifically designed for one method or the other; color laser copiers have a heating element, whereas inkjet printers do not. The papers are not interchangeable, so be sure to check the label carefully.

Read and follow the paper manufacturer's directions for transferring the image; the directions on page 176 are very general. Be sure to reverse or "mirror" the image before printing so that it will transfer to the fabric in the original direction. Use a dry iron heated to the highest setting or a heat press set between 350°F (180°C) and 375°F (190°C) for the transfer process. Another difference among the transfer papers is that some must be peeled away while they are still hot. Others are peeled away after they have cooled. Removing hot-peel paper takes a little dexterity, since the paper backing has to remain hot in order to peel off without damaging the image. The cool-peel papers are easier on your fingers and easier to use. With either paper, try to remove the backing with one continuous motion, peeling in the direction of the fabric grain in order to avoid distortion or unwanted lines in the image.

Transfer photographic images to white fabric for the truest color. Because the transfer is transparent, any color or design in the fabric will affect the image. Fine cotton with a high thread count produces the sharpest image; looser weaves and textures distort the image. However, you may want to experiment with pastels, tiny pale prints, or slight texture if an altered image is part of your creative intention!

Materials

- ◆ Photograph, black and white or color.
- ◆ Photo transfer paper appropriate for method used.
- ◆ Color laser copier or computer, scanner, and color inkjet printer.
- ◆ Iron or heat press.
- ◆ White finely woven cotton fabric, or fabric of choice.

HOW TO TRANSFER A PHOTO TO FABRIC

1 Print photograph or image on transfer paper, using color laser copier; reverse image before printing, so that image will appear normal when transferred to fabric. Or, scan photo, reverse image, and print on transfer paper, using color inkjet printer.

2 Cut away any excess transfer paper or unwanted portions of image. Place fabric, right side up, on firm, lightly padded surface. Place transfer paper, image side down, over fabric. Heat iron to highest setting; do not use steam.

3 Heat fabric with iron; place transfer facedown on fabric, and smooth onto fabric with fingers. Place iron on back of transfer; press down as hard as you can. Hold in one area for up to 30 seconds before moving to another area. Repeat until entire transfer has been pressed; shift angle of iron often to avoid steam vent marks.

4 Press again over entire transfer sheet. For hot-peel paper, lift one corner slightly to check transfer. Immediately peel paper backing in one continuous motion, peeling in the direction of the fabric grain. Allow to cool. For cool-peel paper, allow paper to cool completely before checking transfer and peeling.

Enlarge or reduce photo size as desired before printing. Check to see that increase in size does not distort or blur image by printing on plain paper first.

Economize by scanning or copying several photos at one time. Cut individual images apart after printing onto transfer paper.

Copy several photos onto plain paper. Create an interesting collage by cutting them apart, trimming away unwanted areas, and overlapping images. Then copy collage onto transfer paper.

Print black and white photos in sepia tones for a nostalgic touch, using either the color laser copier or the inkjet printer. Print out the image on plain paper to test first. Or, print a black and white photo on transfer paper, and transfer it to a pastel fabric.

178

Stitched
DESIGNS

With needle and thread as your
paintbrush, translate your creative
ideas into colorful designs,
rich in texture and full of surprise.
Imagine the possibilities!

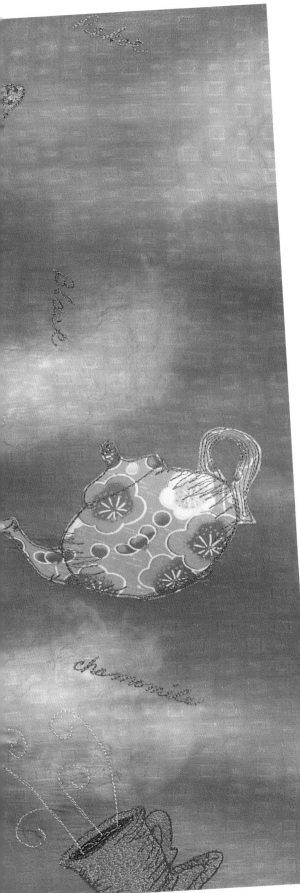

FREE-MOTION EMBROIDERY ▪ ▪ ▪ ▪ ▪

Your sewing machine may be your most valuable and versatile tool for interpreting your inspirations into works of art. Far beyond the utilitarian uses of sewing seams and altering hems, even a basic sewing machine with straight-stitch and zigzag capabilities has the capacity for creating fascinating thread "sketches" and machine embroidered "paintings."

While painted and dyed images offer color, design, and visual depth, machine embroidery goes one step farther, adding wonderful tactile surface texture. With the creative use of thread color, stitch placement, and stitch density, you can stitch outlined sketches, rhythmic flowing lines, or filled-in and shaded images. Free-motion embroidery can accent or repeat the lines of a stamped, stenciled, or screen-printed design. For some appliqué techniques, machine embroidery is both a functional and decorative element of the overall design.

If you can draw or paint, you can learn to use your sewing machine to stitch free-flowing images and designs on fabric. The basic difference is that instead of moving a pencil or paintbrush across a stationary surface, you are moving the surface around under a stationary needle. Even if you think you can't draw or paint, you can undoubtedly trace over a line, in which case you can transfer your design to the fabric first. Like any other skill, once you learn these basic free-motion stitching techniques, the more you practice the better you'll get.

For free-motion machine embroidery, the feed dogs are either covered or lowered, if possible; the stitch length and direction are controlled by the artist. There is usually no need for a presser foot, though a darning foot can be used. Sketching and outlining are usually done with the machine set for a straight stitch. A zigzag stitch can be used for filling in and shading areas. To prevent puckering and help you establish a smooth, flowing motion, you must temporarily stabilize the fabric in some way. Most often, the fabric is held taut in an embroidery hoop. Tear-away stabilizer is used on the wrong side of the fabric for extra stability. Water-soluble stabilizer, used either on the right or wrong side, is useful for fabrics that are washable.

Machine embroidery threads, in cotton, rayon, and metallics, come in a wide array of colors. They vary in weight, from 30-weight to 60-weight, with the lower numbers being the heavier threads. Select needle type and size according to the fabric as well as the thread. Needle sizes 70/9 and 80/11 are suitable for cotton embroidery thread; for rayon and metallic threads, use size 80/11 or 90/14. Fine cotton thread is used in the bobbin, unless the fabric is meant to be decorative on both sides, in which case the same embroidery thread is wound on the bobbin. Run a test sample, and adjust the stitch tension, if necessary.

Keep fabric taut in a ¼" (6 mm) thick embroidery hoop, in a diameter that is easy to work with under the presser foot. Wrap inner ring of wooden hoop with cotton twill tape to protect delicate fabrics.

Place fabric, right side up, over outer ring; push inner ring in place, keeping fabric taut and grainline undistorted. Push inner ring through to underside about ⅛" (3 mm).

Sit directly in front of the machine needle, with hands resting comfortably on sides of hoop; do not grip hoop. Guide fabric with wrist motions, resting elbows on table or on books stacked around bed of machine, so shoulders are not tense.

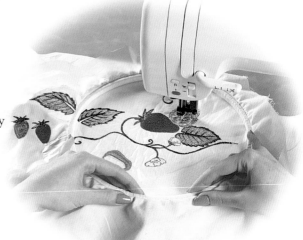

Move the fabric at a smooth, even pace while running machine at moderate to fast speed to obtain short even stitches. Develop skill by writing words; practice loops, circles, or stipple patterns.

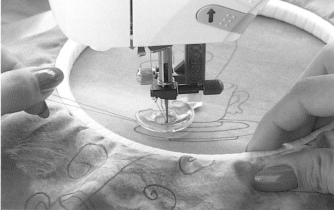

Lower presser foot lever, engaging tension discs. This is easy to overlook when sewing without a presser foot or with a darning foot. Bring bobbin thread through to right side, and hold both threads to one side as you begin stitching. Stitch in place a few times to secure stitches at beginning and end or whenever changing colors.

Adjust tension so that top thread is pulled slightly to underside for fabric with definite "right side." Adjust tension so that stitches look nearly the same from both sides for a reversible look.

Fill in areas using wide zigzag stitch; move fabric side to side, stitching rows directly next to each other. To blend one color into another, leave irregular border; stitch into border at varying depths with adjoining color.

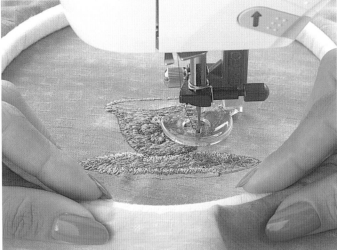

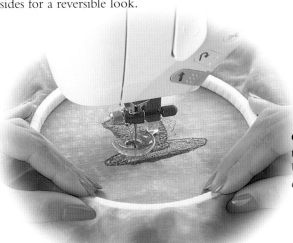

Outline areas with two or three tightly spaced rows of straight stitches. Use the same technique to add design lines to filled-in areas.

Use quilter's gloves or rubber fingertips instead of a hoop when minimal stabilizing is required or when you want to stitch freely over wide spans of fabric without breaking the stitching line.

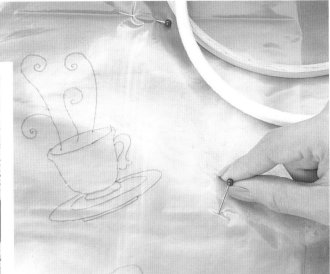

Mark design on water-soluble stabilizer, and pin it to fabric surface, if desired.

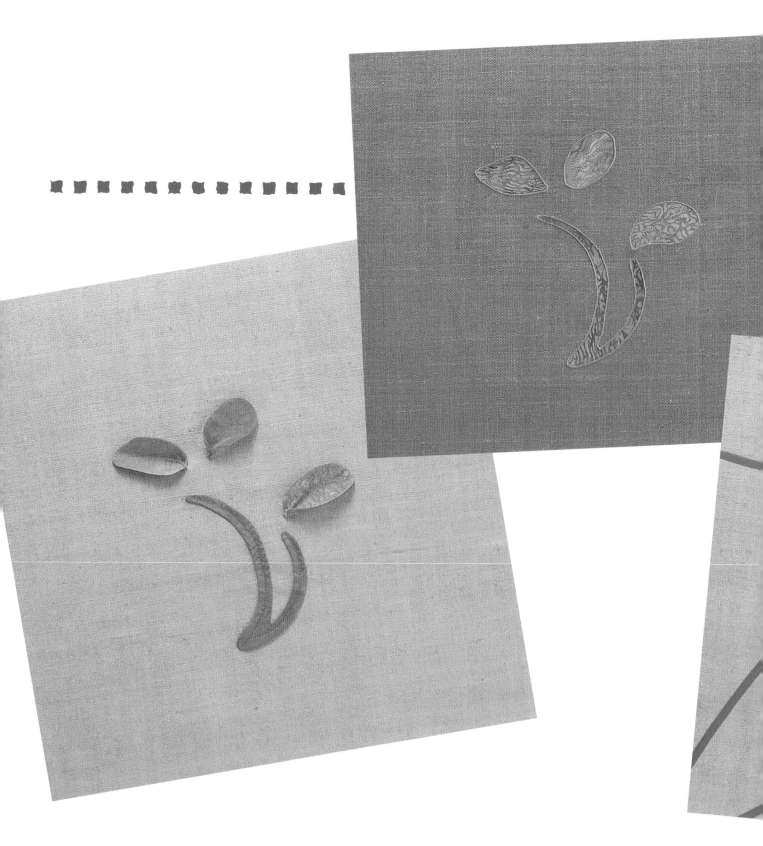

APPLIQUÉ

Many fabric artists incorporate some form of appliqué into their creations, thus adding color and design with the bonus of textural interest. In simple terms, an appliqué is a fabric cutout attached to the surface of a larger piece of fabric. However, a fabric cutout can be interpreted in countless ways, from a single shape to a complex puzzle of interacting shapes. An appliqué can be a photographic image transferred to fabric or a stenciled design that is lined and beaded. It may not even be fabric at all, but rather a unique found object that is incorporated into the surface design of the fabric.

Equally as endless are the possible methods for attaching that appliqué to the surface. Satin-stitched appliqué is certainly a viable option, and one that is often appropriate. However, there are many other methods of application that are effective and appropriate in the right circumstances. The key is to attach the appliqué in a way that is consistent with the form and function of the item being created while complementing both the appliqué and the surrounding fabric.

These examples and brief descriptions give you a glimpse at the possibilities. Some methods are taught in more detail on the pages that follow.

Forms of Appliqué

1 **Raw-edge appliqué** (page 188). Edges of the cutout are not finished or turned under. The cutout may be secured with straight stitches, multistitch-zigzag, or free-motion stitching. Because the edges are not emphasized, the cutout seems to merge with the background fabric.

2 **Satin-stitched appliqué.** Tightly spaced zigzag stitches form a small ridge around the cutout, accenting the edges and giving the appliqué prominence.

3 **Couched appliqué.** Cutouts are secured by couching a decorative cord around the outer edge, creating a ridge and finishing the cut edges.

4 **Lined appliqué** (page 192). Each cutout is lined to the edge. Pieces can be applied to lie flat on the surface or secured with internal stitches that allow the edges to rise, revealing the lining and creating a three-dimensional effect.

5 **Negative appliqué** (page 195). Background fabric is cut away in desired shapes to reveal contrasting fabric layered underneath. Cut edges can be treated in a variety of ways to make the appliqué blend into the background fabric or create depth or dimension.

6 **Bias strip appliqué** (page 199). Tubes or strips of fabric are secured to a background fabric, creating raised designs. Knots, beads, or other interesting objects may be incorporated.

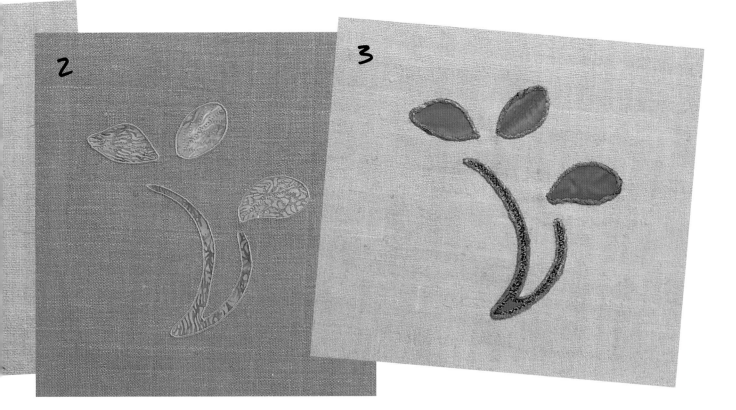

187

RAW-EDGE APPLIQUÉ

There are many styles of raw-edge appliqué, most of them conforming to a few basic principles. Shapes are usually cut free-hand, though an artist may get inspiration from a printed design and may even draw shapes onto the fabric before cutting. In some styles, motifs are cut from printed fabric and applied as appliqués to another background fabric. Fabrics are usually firm and closely woven because the cut edges are neither finished nor turned under. Appliqué edges will fray slightly in wearing and laundering, softening the design edges. Nonwoven fabrics provide clean edges that will not fray and require little sewing. Almost anything, including nets, laces, fringed selvages, and scraps of needlework may be used to achieve certain design effects.

Hold motifs in place temporarily with pins or with wash-away adhesive spray. Then secure the appliqué with a machine-guided straight stitch or multistitch-zigzag, changing stitch length and width to create interest. Use free-motion thread sketching for a very effective method of attachment. Choose thread color to match the fabric for inconspicuous stitching. Add or amplify design details by using contrasting colors and shades of thread. Select a bobbin thread to match the background fabric, and adjust the tension, if necessary, to prevent the bobbin thread from coming to the surface. Launder the fabric after applying the appliqué to gently fray the edges and give the entire appliqué a softer appearance.

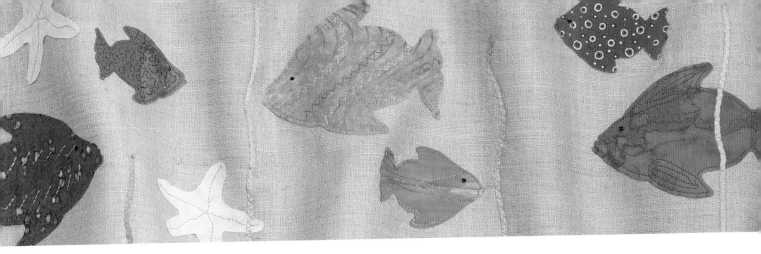

INDIVIDUAL MOTIFS

1 Cut shapes from selected fabrics. Arrange on the background fabric; secure temporarily to the background fabric using adhesive spray, pins, or glue stick.

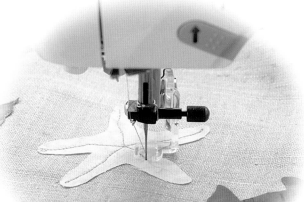

2 Stitch to background fabric, using machine-guided or free-motion edgestitching for a flat design. Secure with interior stitches along design lines for a more dimensional effect. Stitch interior design lines, as desired.

PRINT MOTIF APPLIQUÉ

1 Cut motifs from printed fabric and reposition them on the background fabric in a new arrangement. For instance, create a border print with motifs cut from an all-over print fabric. Secure temporarily.

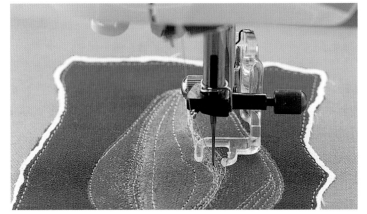

2 Secure with free-motion stitching ⅛" (3 mm) from cut edges. Stitch free-motion thread sketching (page 181) to interiors of motifs to soften and blend colors and emphasize design details. For textural interest, couch decorative cords or yarns over strong design lines.

2 Add patches of color, one at a time, overlapping as necessary to build design. Stitch appropriate pattern in each patch.

1 Plan your design, drawing inspiration from a photograph or painting, perhaps. Cut amorphous patches of various sizes from solid colors or muted prints to roughly represent elements of the design. Position patch for most recessed element of design on background fabric; secure temporarily. Stitch over patch, using free-motion technique in a pattern that resembles the element you want to convey. For instance, circles over a blue patch suggest a clump of grapes. Trim edges.

FABRIC COLLAGE ▨ ▨ ▨ ▨

1 Working from a photograph or painting, select a multitude of fabrics with small patterns in different colors and values to achieve a painterly effect. Convert the photograph to a line drawing; cut shapes to represent all the divisions in the drawing.

2 Layer pieces on background fabric to fill in the design; secure temporarily. Secure pieces, using free-motion stitching, or multistitch-zigzag.

3 Add shading and accent design lines with free-motion thread sketching, satin stitching, or couched yarns.

LINED APPLIQUÉ

Lined appliqués are completely finished around the outer edge before they are attached to the background fabric. Any fabric is a candidate for the appliqué fabric, as long as its character and color provide the desired effect. Delicate or loosely woven fabrics can be stabilized with lightweight fusible knit interfacing, giving them added body and minimizing fraying around the closely trimmed edges.

Suitable lining fabric varies, depending on the method of attachment. The appliqué can be attached by invisibly blindstitching around the outer edge. Using this method, the lining is entirely hidden, and therefore any sheer or lightweight tightly woven fabric is suitable. Tulle netting works well because it does not ravel and it allows you the extra advantage of being able to see through the lining when positioning it on the fabric. Tulle lining also enables you to use sheer fabric or lace for the appliqué, opening up a new realm of possibilities.

Another method of attachment utilizes stitched design lines on the interior of the appliqué. With this method, the outer edge of the appliqué rises from the surface, creating more dimension and exposing the lining to some degree. A sculpted effect can be created by manipulating the appliqué into a raised and shaped form before securing it with internal stitches. For these techniques, you may want to select either self fabric or a coordinating lightweight fabric for the lining, incorporating it into your overall design.

HOW TO SEW A LINED APPLIQUÉ

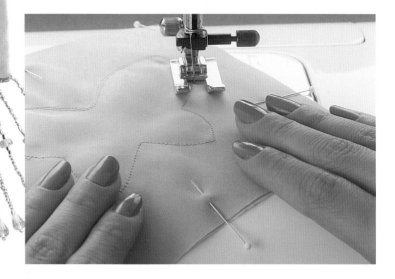

1 Trace desired shape onto wrong side of lining fabric. Place lining fabric over appliqué fabric, right sides together; pin. Stitch all around design, using short stitches. Stitch again just outside first row of stitches.

2 Trim close to second stitching line. Cut small slit in lining, away from outer edge. If appliqué is dimensional, slit lining in area that will not be exposed.

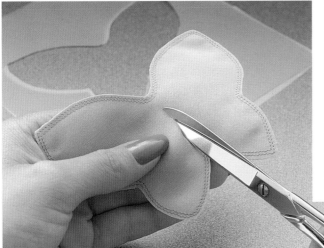

3 Turn appliqué right side out through slit. Push out any curves or points, using narrow, blunt tool, such as a cuticle stick; press.

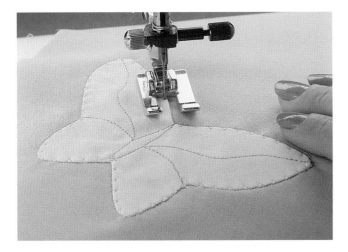

4 **Blindstitch method.** Stitch any internal design lines. Pin appliqué to background fabric. Thread machine with invisible nylon thread; blindstitch on background fabric as close to appliqué as possible, just catching appliqué edge with left-hand swing of needle.

4 **Dimensional method.** Stitch any internal design lines not intended to secure appliqué. Secure appliqué to background fabric along remaining internal design lines, hiding slit in lining.

4 **Sculpted method.** Stitch any internal design lines not intended to secure appliqué. Manipulate appliqué as desired; secure to background fabric with additional stitching on internal design lines.

NEGATIVE APPLIQUÉ ·········

Unlike other methods in which appliqués are sewn on top of the surface fabric, negative appliqué methods involve the removal of surface fabric to reveal appliqué fabric layered underneath. The technique may be as simple as cutting openings in the top fabric and treating the cut edges in a manner similar to raw-edge appliqué (page 188). In another technique, called shuttered windows, geometric openings are partially cut in the surface fabric, and excess fabric flaps are secured to one side. This method adds dimension to the surface and offers tantalizing peeks into the fabric beneath it. Faced openings have a finished edge all around the opening, providing a dramatic framework for showcasing interesting printed designs or photo transfers (page 174) perhaps. To further enhance the appliqué, a contrasting facing is rolled slightly to the right side, resembling the matting in framed artwork.

HOW TO SEW RAW-EDGE NEGATIVE APPLIQUÉS ▪ ▪ ▪ ▪ ▪ ▪ ▪ ▪

1 Cut openings in surface fabric; discard cutouts. Spray wrong side of surface fabric with temporary fabric adhesive. Place appliqué fabrics facedown over openings on wrong side of surface fabric.

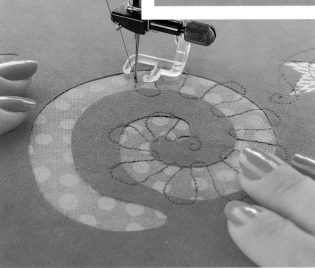

2 Stitch over openings from right side, using desired stitching techniques such as free-motion stippling or thread sketching or machine-guided decorative stitches.

2 Cut all but one side of opening, leaving fabric flap; pin flap to side of shape. Stitch over previous stitches, using satin stitches or embroidery pattern.

1 Mark desired straight-edged geometric openings on surface fabric. Cut on one side. Layer over appliqué fabric; stitch around each marked opening, using short straight stitches just outside marked lines.

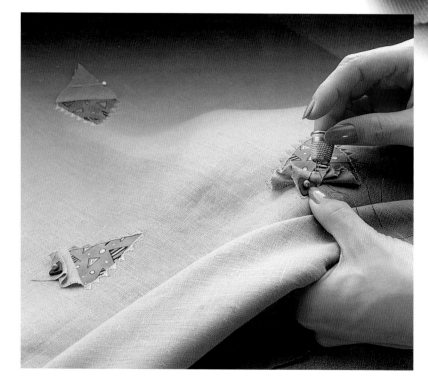

3 Roll, pleat, or gather flap back away from opening. Tack in place or secure with hand-stitched bead.

1 Cut facing fabric at least 1" (2.5 cm) larger than intended opening. Cut appliqué of same size. Draw opening on wrong side of facing; place over surface fabric in desired location, right sides together. Stitch around marked opening, using short straight stitches. Stitch again within opening, next to first stitches.

2 Trim away facing and surface fabric ⅛" (3 mm) inside inner stitched line; clip curves and into corners up to stitches.

3 Turn facing to inside; press, rolling facing slightly to right side, if desired. Turn surface fabric over. Pin appliqué to facing, right sides together. Stitch ¼" (6 mm) from edges, keeping surface fabric out of the way.

4 Embellish appliqué, if desired. On right side of surface fabric, stitch around outside of opening through all layers, using decorative stitch or free-motion stitching.

BIAS STRIP APPLIQUÉ ●●●●●

Quilters commonly use bias tape or tubes to create quilts with stained glass or Celtic designs. The same techniques can easily be used to embellish fabric for clothing or home decorating projects. Prefolded fusible bias tape, available in several colors and metallics, makes quick work of intricate designs. Cut and sew bias tube appliqués from other fabrics, using convenient tools, such as the Fasturn®, for turning tubes right side out, and flat aluminum or nylon press bars, if flat strips with pressed folds are desired.

Depending on the look you want, select one of several methods for sewing the appliqué to the background fabric. Straight-stitch along the outer edges or sew decorative stitches down the center of flattened appliqué strips. For a raised effect, make tubes from fabric with more body, such as wool crepe, and attach them with invisible machine or hand stitches. Shape them into tight curves, entwine or braid them into intricate designs, tie knots, or add beads for more dimension.

To determine the bias length needed for intricate designs, draw the design to size on paper. Tape the end of a string to a starting point in the design; trail the string over the design, following the lines until the entire pattern is complete. Then measure the total length of string used. Allow extra length for any knots and for maneuvering the tube to hide seams. Bias strips up to 65" (165.5 cm) long can be cut from the true bias of 45" (115 cm) fabric. For large complex designs, it may be easier to work with shorter lengths, hiding cut ends under intersections in the design.

◼ ◼ HOW TO APPLY A FUSIBLE BIAS TAPE DESIGN ◼ ◼ ◼

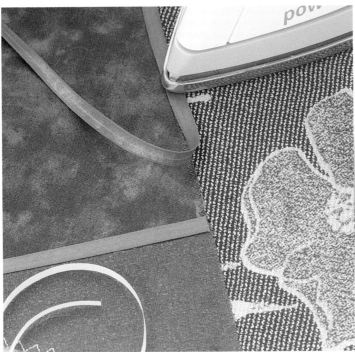

2 Edgestitch along both edges of tape. Or stitch down center of tape, using multistitch-zigzag or decorative machine stitch.

1 Mark design on right side of fabric. Stabilize background fabric, using desired method. Remove protective backing and fuse bias tape over design lines, working in small sections.

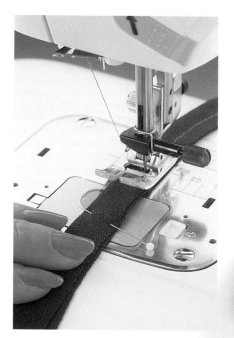

2 Turn tube right side out, using Fasturn or another suitable tool. For flattened tube, insert press bar into tube to manipulate tube into consistent width; press, keeping seam on back of tube. Move bar through tube until entire tube is pressed.

1 Cut bias strip desired finished width plus ½" (1.3 cm). Fold in half; stitch ¼" (6 mm) from edges, forming tube.

3 Mark design and stabilize background fabric. Arrange tube on design lines, securing as necessary with fabric glue or pins. Knot tube or add beads in desired positions.

4 Place fabric facedown over a light box. Secure tube, stitching by hand from wrong side, along center of tube.

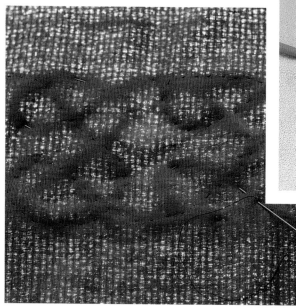

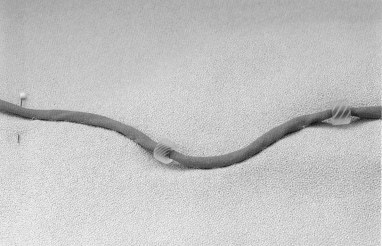

Machine-stitched method. Blindstitch along one or both sides of tube, using invisible nylon thread. If tube crosses *under* itself, jump intersection; secure threads by stitching in place for several stitches before and after intersection. If tube crosses *over* itself, continue blindstitching through intersection. Leave short lengths of tube unstitched before and after knots and beads.

Cover end with another appliqué.

Turn under tape end before stitching. Turn in ends of tube; hand-stitch closed.

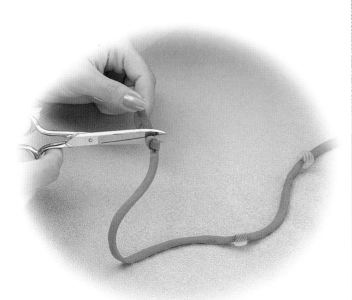

Knot tube end; trim close. Allow several inches (centimeters) to hang free from background fabric, if desired.

Plan appliqué ends to be caught in seams of project.

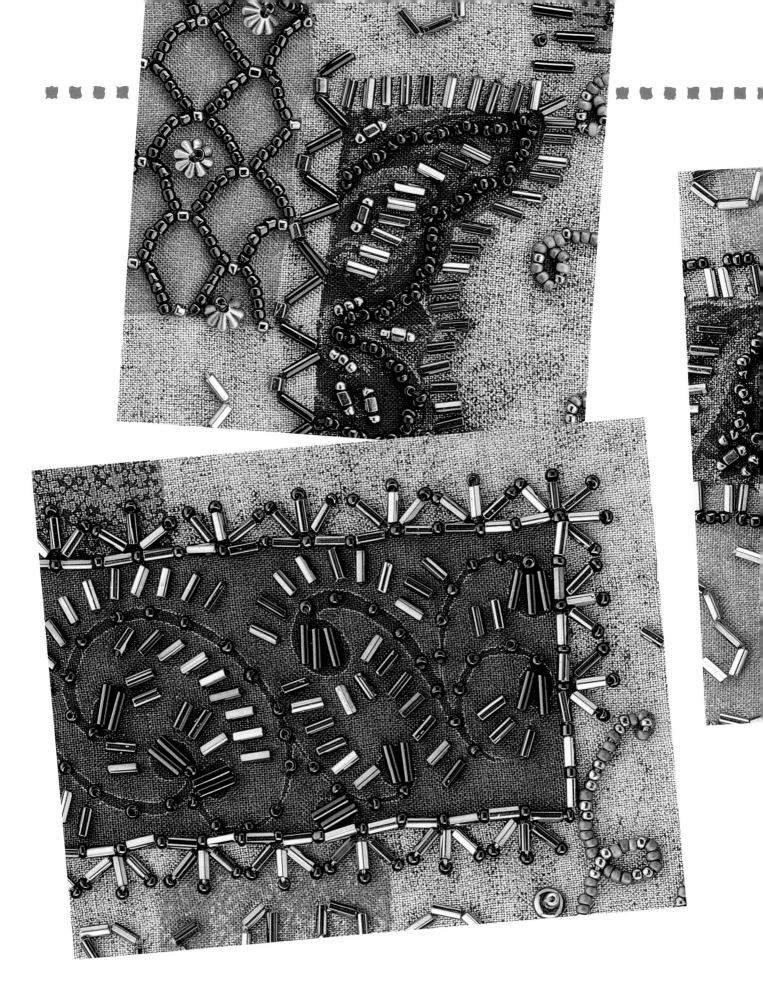

BEADWORK ON FABRIC

Beadwork punctuates the surface of a fabric with texture and dazzling color. A heavily beaded design creates a focal point on a garment or quilt, while beads dispersed broadly over the fabric surface serve as a subtle accent. Beaded patterns may follow a transferred design of your choice or be incorporated into the fabric print.

Both machine sewing and hand stitching techniques are used for beadwork. Machine sewing is used to couch strung beads onto fabric for outlining, edging, or free-form lines. Loose beads are hand-sewn to fabric individually, in clusters or rows, or using specialty stitches to create intriguing dimensional effects. It is also possible to machine-stitch individual beads with holes large enough to accommodate the machine needle. This makes it possible to incorporate beads into free-motion machine embroidery. With experimentation, the possibilities are limitless. Even the basic stitches shown here can be used to produce a wide range of beaded effects.

Heavily beaded fabric will probably shrink in the beading process, so finish the beadwork before cutting out pieces for the project. Delay beading close to seamlines until the project is complete, allowing room for the presser foot to sew seams. Avoid beading in areas of high friction, such as under the arms on a garment.

The safest way to clean beaded fabric is to wash by hand and lay flat to dry. The clothes dryer inevitably chips, breaks, or melts beads. Dry-cleaning solvents can discolor or destroy some beads. Make a small sample with the beads and thread you intend to use in the project, and wash or dry-clean it, checking the beads for colorfastness and durability.

Beads are a choking hazard for small children, who are attracted to shiny colored objects. If children will be near your work area, be sure to put away beads when you are done working. Do not apply beads to clothing or accessories used by children.

Identifying Beads

Beads can be made of almost any material, including glass, plastic, polymer clay, shell, bone, wood, ceramic, metal, precious and semiprecious stone, and paper. The appropriateness of the beads for any project depends not only on their size, shape, and color, but also their weight and cleaning methods. For instance, while glass beads are the most common, they also are much heavier than plastic, paper, or wood, which is something to consider for a heavily beaded garment.

Beads are categorized according to their shape. Seed beads **(1)** are small and round, with a center hole. They are sold loose or on cotton strings, intended to be sewn separately or transferred to stronger beading thread for couching onto fabric. Bugle beads **(2)** are tubular, ranging in length from 2 to 4 mm. Drops **(3)** are pear-shaped, with a hole at the narrow end or lengthwise through the bead. Faceted beads **(4),** often transparent, have flat surfaces that are cut or molded. Roundels **(5)** are flat, doughnut-shaped beads. Fancy beads **(6)** of various shapes, sizes, materials, and hole placements have a wide range of decorative uses. Strung beads, for couching onto fabric, include rhinestones **(7),** molded plastic pearls **(8),** and cross-locked glass beads **(9).** The methods used for stringing them vary, but all are intended to keep the beads from coming apart when the string is cut.

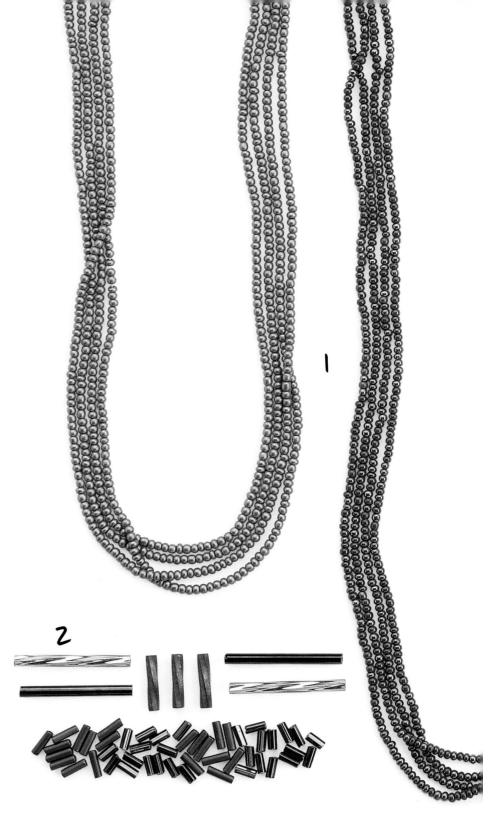

3

4

5

6

9

7

8

Beading Supplies

Beading needles **(1),** thinner and more flexible than standard hand-sewing needles, are available in sizes 10 to 14; the larger the number, the smaller the needle. They are usually sold in packs of twenty-five, a convenience due to their fragile nature.

Prewaxed twisted nylon beading thread **(2)** works well for most hand-sewn projects. A double strand of waxed cotton–wrapped polyester thread **(3)** is also recommended. Match the thread to the fabric, if you are using multiple colors of opaque beads. Transparent or semitransparent beads will be affected by the thread color. For machine sewing, use thread appropriate for the fabric and the technique. For instance, when beading is worked into free-motion embroidery, use cotton, rayon, or metallic embroidery thread **(4).** Use invisible nylon thread **(5)** for couching strung beads.

Beading bobbins **(6),** most commonly in sizes B and D, are wound with fine waxed nylon cord. They are used for hand sewing or for stringing beads before couching onto fabric, and are not intended to be inserted into the bobbin case of your sewing machine. The cord sticks to itself, unwinding as it is needed.

Liquid fray preventer **(7)** is useful for sealing knots on the underside of the fabric. Clear nail polish may also be used, but will leave a mark if it touches the fabric.

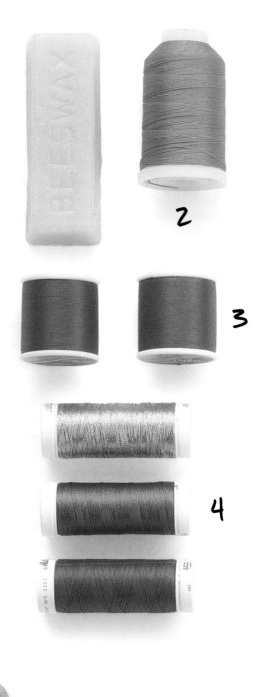

8

9

10

11

12

13

Many beaders swear by the use of corduroy fabric **(8)**, sorting and arranging the beads between the wales.

Needle-nose pliers **(9)** are indispensable for pulling needles through stubborn beads, or breaking off disfigured beads or those mistakenly sewn in the wrong place. Tweezers **(10)** are great for holding individual or strung beads in place to be stitched with the sewing machine.

If you intend to fill an area heavily with beadwork, stabilize the fabric to prevent it from puckering and shrinking up from all the stitches, and to help it retain its original grainlines. If the area to be beaded is too large to fit entirely in an embroidery hoop **(11)** or scroll frame **(12)**, attach the fabric to a stretcher bar frame **(13)** of any size. Use water-soluble stabilizer for lightweight, lightly beaded fabric that must retain its drape after beading. Stabilize heavily beaded fabric on the underside with fusible interfacing.

Select design-transfer materials and methods suitable for your project. A favorite method is to trace the design on water-soluble stabilizer and secure it to the right side of the fabric, thus providing the design markings and stabilizing the fabric at the same time.

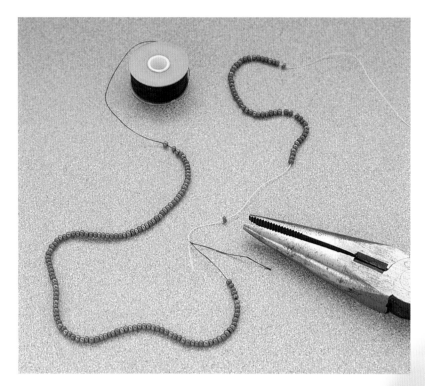

Attach beading foot or piping foot to conventional machine to sew over strung beads. The grooved bottom must be deep enough to allow presser foot to ride over beads without rubbing. Adjust zigzag length so one complete zigzag stitch is equal to distance between beads. Adjust stitch width so needle stitches over beads without hitting them.

Transfer beads from weak cotton thread onto beading bobbin before stitching to fabric. Knot threads together; slide beads from cotton thread onto bobbin thread. Break off any beads that will not slide over knot, using needle-nose pliers. Cut off cotton thread at knot; do not cut bobbin thread. Bobbin will unwind as needed.

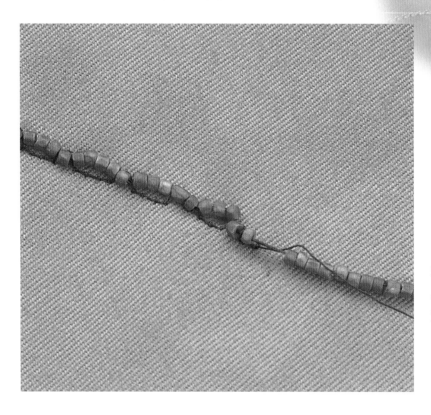

Alternate method. Set machine for blindhem stitch, so that straight stitches align to the right side of the strung beads and left-hand stitch jumps over string between two beads.

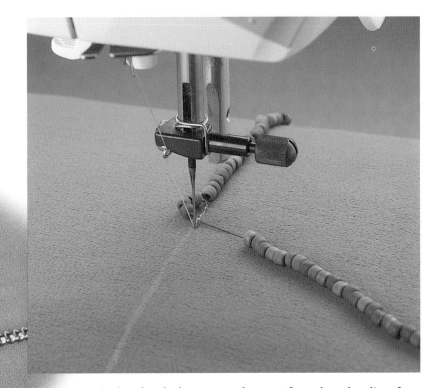

String beads that are too large to fit under a beading foot onto beading bobbin (opposite); secure end to wrong side. Stitch in free motion along intended path; trail beads to one side ahead of needle. Move bead string from one side to the other every few stitches, stitching across string, to hold beads in place. Snug beads back before each crossing.

Secure cross-locked beads at ends of rows by removing several beads and knotting threads close to last bead; thread tails through needle and pull to wrong side. Most other types of strung beads can be cut without raveling.

Attach beading foot to serger. Use mono-filament nylon thread in right needle and loopers. Adjust stitch length to match bead size. Set machine for desired stitch: rolled hem (top) lays beads off edge, for reversible finish; 3-thread overlock (center) lays beads on finished fabric edge; flatlocking on a fold (bottom) couches beading in straight lines across the fabric surface.

HOW TO ATTACH INDIVIDUAL BEADS ▪▫▪▫▪▫▪▫▪▫▪ WITH FREE-MOTION MACHINE STITCHING

1 Lower or cover feed dogs; remove presser foot. Set machine for straight stitch. Draw bobbin thread to right side of fabric at desired starting point. Stitch several tiny stitches; stop. Trim off thread tails.

2 Hold bead, hole up, one bead length away from thread exit point, using tweezers. Move fabric under needle until tip aligns to hole. Slowly guide needle down through bead hole; release bead and complete stitch.

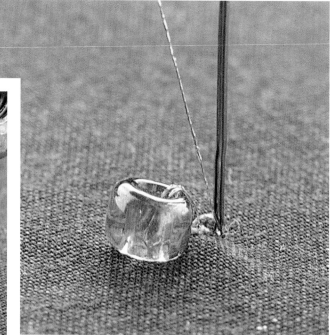

3 Insert needle into original thread exit point; complete stitch. Stitch to next desired bead location, if stitch trail is desirable or invisible. Or tie off threads and move to new position, starting again with step 1.

Stop stitch. Bring needle up through primary bead and seed bead on right side of fabric; seed bead is called the "stop." Bring needle back through primary bead, then down through fabric to wrong side. This stitch is frequently used for attaching single large beads, or a bugle bead that stands on end, or a roundel.

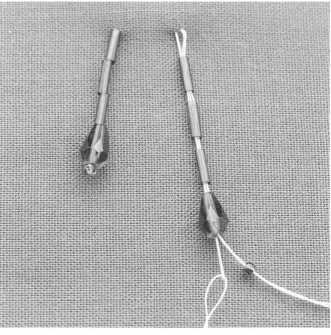

Dangle stitch. Bring needle up through several beads on right side of fabric; the last bead, or the stop, is usually a small seed bead. Bring needle back through all beads except the stop bead, then down through fabric to wrong side. Knot thread on wrong side after each dangle stitch. This stitch is frequently used to create fringe.

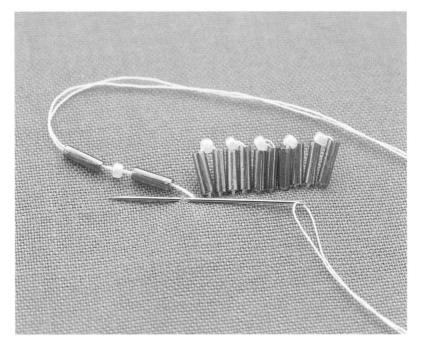

Fence stitch. Bring needle up through a bugle bead, a seed bead, and a second bugle bead. Take a short stitch so bugle beads stand on end. Repeat the stitch, creating the fence effect.

(continued)

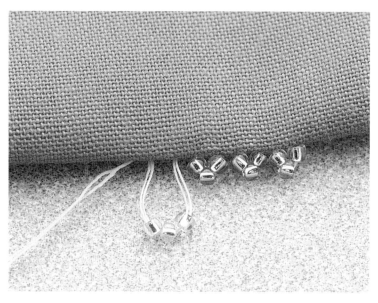

Edging stitch. Bring needle up through three seed beads. Take a short stitch so first and last beads rest next to each other; middle bead is suspended between them.

Backstitch. Bring needle up through three seed beads; slide beads down thread to fabric surface. Insert needle back through fabric at end of third bead; bring needle back up through fabric between first and second beads, running needle also through second and third beads. Add three beads to needle and repeat stitches. This is a secure stitch for sewing beads in a continuous line.

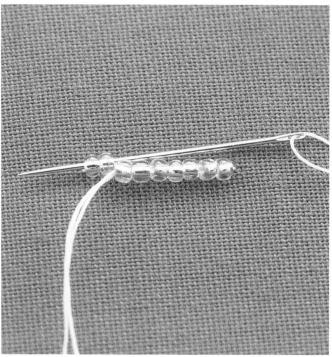

Filling stitch. Bring needle up through several beads, actual number determined by width of space to fill in. Slide beads down thread to fabric surface; insert needle back through fabric at end of last bead. Bring needle back up through fabric next to last bead; add several beads to needle and insert needle back through fabric next to first bead of previous row. Repeat, working closely spaced rows to fill in an area.

NET-WEAVING ON FABRIC

Stitch a grid of beadwork on fabric to create an interesting border, fill in an isolated area, or accent the lines of a printed or woven check. To develop the rhythm of the stitch, it is easiest to work on an evenly spaced grid, either transferred to fabric or innate in the fabric's weave or print. The beaded lines of the grid float on the fabric surface, so it is recommended that, if the finished project will be handled or worn, the lines include no more than ten seed beads each. At each intersecting corner, a "point bead" is secured to the fabric, holding the entire grid in place.

Work the grid back and forth in zigzagging rows that run horizontally or vertically. Each row must have the same even number of point beads; the last point bead in each row becomes the first point bead in the next row. For additional accents, secure unique beads in some of the squares of the grid.

HOW TO NET-WEAVE ON FABRIC

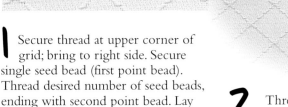

1 Secure thread at upper corner of grid; bring to right side. Secure single seed bead (first point bead). Thread desired number of seed beads, ending with second point bead. Lay beads along diagonal grid line; secure second point bead at second corner.

2 Thread same number of seed beads as in step 1; end with third point bead. Lay beads along next grid line in a zigzag pattern. Secure point bead. Repeat to end of grid row. Begin second row, angling back in opposite direction, and securing point bead at fourth corner of last square.

3 Thread same number of seed beads as between all other point beads. Lay beads on grid line, closing square. Secure to fabric, running needle through point bead and fabric. Continue second row, adding new point beads only to corners that do not join first row. Continue net-weaving until desired grid is complete.

TRANSFERRING DESIGNS & MARKING FABRIC ▪▪▪▪▪▪▪

Decorative stitching techniques often require you to mark design guidelines on the surface of your fabric. Browse the latest sewing notions catalogs or walk through the notions department of any fabric store and you will realize that the number of products for transferring designs and marking fabric are staggering. Depending on the fabric and sewing technique you are using, you may find some products to be more useful and appropriate than others. The product should be easy to use, highly visible, and easily removable in a manner consistant with your fabric's care needs. For instance, a water-soluble marking pen is only suitable for marking on washable fabrics and trims.

Transferring methods vary, also, depending on the density and surface texture of the fabric. A light box is a handy tool for lightweight and light-colored fabrics that are easily penetrated by light. Heavy fabrics and dark-colored fabrics can be marked using other methods, such as transfer paper or netting. Highly textured fabrics may require some innovative marking methods, such as freezer paper or thread sketching. When transferring a design, keep in mind that if you will be stitching from the wrong side of the fabric, the mirror image of the design will appear on the right side.

It is a good idea to purchase a variety of marking tools to give yourself options. Always test the marking method and removal on a scrap of your fabric before using it on your project.

Water-erasable and air-erasable marking pens are available with fine points for intricate marking. Water-erasable marks disappear with a few drops of water; air-erasable marks vanish in 12 to 24 hours.

Soapstone marker can be sharpened to a fine point for intricate marking. Soapstone rubs off easily and is safe for all fibers.

Marking Tools

White water-soluble pencil, handy for marking on dark fabrics, disappears with a few drops of cold water.

Quilter's pencils, available in white, yellow, or gray lead, have eraser ends for easy removal. Some are mechanical, with lead refills. Leads are oil-free and contain less graphite to prevent smearing.

ULTIMATE FOR QUI

Transfer paper. Select wax-free, carbonless transfer paper in color that will be visible on your fabric. Place fabric on smooth surface with appropriate side up. Place transfer paper facedown over fabric; place design over transfer paper. Secure with weights or pins. Trace simple designs with tracing wheel. Trace intricate designs with stylus or empty ballpoint pen. Trace design lines in systematic order, to ensure that all lines are traced before lifting design and transfer paper.

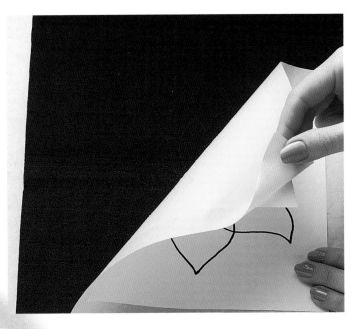

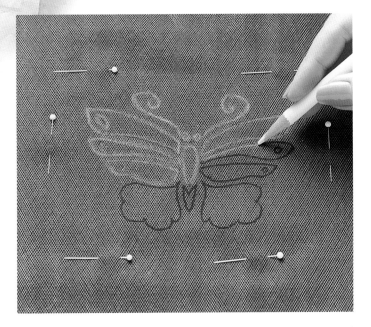

Water-soluble stabilizer. Trace design onto water-soluble stabilizer. Position stabilizer over right side of fabric; pin. Stitch over design lines, using free-motion stitching techniques (page 192). Remove stabilizer, if desired. Or leave stabilizer in place until decorative stitching is complete; then remove it. This method is especially useful for highly textured fabric.

Netting. Trace design onto nylon netting, using permanent marker. Position netting over fabric; pin. Transfer design by marking over netting with appropriate marking tool.

(continued)

Light box. Trace design onto tracing paper, if necessary, using bold, dark lines. Tape design on light box surface. Position fabric over design as desired; tape. Transfer design, using appropriate marking tool.

Make an inexpensive light box from a clear plastic storage box with a smooth, flat bottom. Purchase a fluorescent light stick that will fit inside.

Trace quilting stencils for continuous background quilting (pages 64 to 67) or decorative bobbin stitching (page 88). Several design variations can be adapted from one stencil.

Tear-away stabilizer. Transfer *mirror image* of design to tear-away stabilizer or dull side of freezer paper. Position stabilizer on wrong side of fabric; pin. Or press freezer paper, shiny side down, to wrong side of fabric. Stitch over design with decorative bobbin stitching.

■ ■ ■ HOW TO DRAW A MIRROR-IMAGE CORNER ■ ■ ■

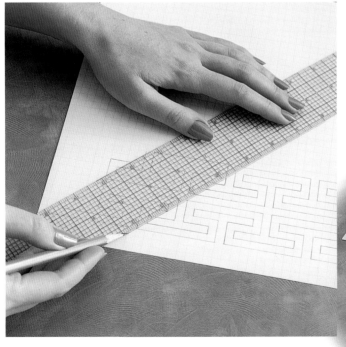

2 Place a rectangular mirror on the angle line, perpendicular to the graph paper. On another piece of graph paper, draw the corner as you see it in the mirror.

1 Draw the design on graph paper. Determine the location at which you want the design to turn the corner and the angle of the corner. Draw a line through the design at the determined angle.

STABILIZERS ▪▪▪▪▪▪▪▪▪▪▪▪▪▪▪▪▪▪

Many of the decorative stitching techniques utilized by fabric artists require that the fabric be stabilized in some way during the stitching process. Stabilizing provides optimum stitch quality without distortion and prevents the fabric from puckering. An assortment of products are available, each designed for various fabrics and sewing techniques. Read and follow the manufacturer's directions and make a test sample, to be sure that the product is right for your fabric and technique.

RinsAway™
WATER SOLUBLE BACKING

Tear-Easy
The Professional's Choice
Soft, Light Tear Stabi

Palmer Pletsch
PerfectSew
WASH-AWAY
FABRIC STABILIZER
Eliminates puckering on:
• machine embroidery
• applique • pintucks • bias
• edges • knit fabrics
• heirloom sewing
• application and
• reuse in
• reuse if diluted

SULLIVANS

FABRIC STABILIZER
• HOLDS FABRIC FIRM
• FOR MACHINE EMBROIDERY • BATTENBURG •
• LACE MAKING • BATTENBURG •
• HEIRLOOM SEWING • APPLIQUE •
• BRUSHES OUT COMPLETELY

• WASHABLE. HARMFUL IF INHALED
• USE UNDER PRESSURE
• (see cautions on back panel)
14 oz. (400G) NET

$ 3.50
Item No. 840-01
Heat-Away™
Brush Off Stabilizer

Heat with iron ⟷ Brush off

Special heat-sensitive woven fabric that disintegrates with a hot iron, then brushes away easily. It's like muslin that vanishes.

Great for:
• Decorative Stitching
• Monogramming
• Battenburg Lace
• Cut Work & Edges
• Lace Work
• Buttonholes
• Machine Embroidery
• 3-D Applique
• Special Effects
• Delicate Fabrics
• Corduroy & Velvet

sulky

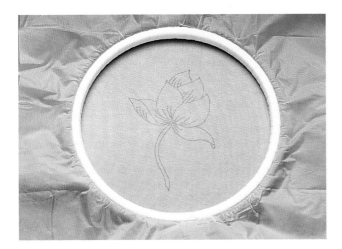

Water-soluble stabilizers, available as transparent films or lightweight fabrics, are designed to be used on either side of the fabric. They can be placed under the fabric like tear-away stabilizers. Or designs can be drawn on water-soluble stabilizer and sewn from the right side of the fabric. Some brands disappear with a light spray of water; others require soaking, making them suitable for washable fabrics only. Embroidery hoops and rings are often used, alone or with other stabilizers, to keep the fabric taut while stitching.

Liquid stabilizers stiffen the fabric itself, much like starch. They are either sprayed onto the fabric or spread on with a soft paintbrush and allowed to dry. Drying time can be shortened by using a hair dryer or pressing with a press cloth and hot iron. After stitching, the stabilizer is washed out of the fabric.

Tear-away stabilizers are placed under the fabric for techniques like machine embroidery and appliqué, when the stitching is done on the right side of the fabric. After stitching, the stabilizer is easily torn away. Any stabilizer trapped under stitches must be left there and, with some products, may wash out during laundering of the garment. Tear-away stabilizer is available in sheets or on rolls, as a paper product or a synthetic. Some brands are thinner than others, designed for very lightweight fabrics. Two or more layers of stabilizer may be necessary to achieve the desired stability. Another brand, designed for knits and slippery wovens, is temporarily heat-fused to the fabric before stitching. Household products like coffee filters, typing paper, freezer paper, or adding machine tape can also be used as tear-away stabilizers.

Heat-sensitive stabilizers brush or flake away when they are pressed with a hot, dry iron. Suitable for thread lace (page 96) or other nondimensional work, heat-sensitive stabilizers can be used on the right or wrong side of mediumweight fabric.

219

INDEX ■■■■■■■■■■■■